SHE RODE MADLY OFF IN ALL DIRECTIONS

Rosie Rollins

Gotham Books

30 N Gould St.
Ste. 20820, Sheridan, WY 82801
https://gothambooksinc.com/

Phone: 1 (307) 464-7800

© 2023 *Rosie Rollins*. All rights reserved.

No part of this book may be reproduced, stored in a retrieval system, or transmitted by any means without the written permission of the author.

Published by Gotham Books (November 29,2023)

ISBN: 979-8-88775-440-6 (P)
ISBN: 979-8-88775-441-3 (E)

Because of the dynamic nature of the Internet, any web addresses or links contained in this book may have changed since publication and may no longer be valid.

The views expressed in this work are solely those of the author and do not necessarily reflect the views of the publisher, and the publisher hereby disclaims any responsibility for them.

TABLE OF CONTENTS

C & O CANAL RIDE 1

THE TEVIS 36

ROCKY MOUNTAIN RIDE 46

NIGHT OF THE CLOUDY MOON 53

ONE OF MY BEST RIDES 63

2003 WESTERN ADVENTURE 69

SANDHILLS RIDE BY HORSEBACK (2009) 86

CENTENNIAL TRAIL RIDE : SOUTH DAKOTA 103

100 MILE RIDES: THE TEVIS & THE OLD DOMINION 125

THE PERFECT CAMP AKA CAMPING WITH BERNICE 130

AUTHOR'S NOTE

In the search for a motto that fits me, I settled on one by an anonymous writer, "She flung herself upon her horse and rode madly off in all directions." Perfect. The following horse adventures were all done by me, and the stories were written by me. Ah, the memories! All wonderful adventures to be shared with readers, some of whom would have loved to take these same rides on horseback. The pictures are from each adventure that follows, some from back in 1965 and on through 2009. I dedicate this publication to all the very special horses who made these adventures possible: Zorro, Blu, Cloudy Moon, and Maple.

C & O CANAL RIDE

I UNDERTOOK THIS ADVENTURE IN 1965.
COPYRIGHT 2012 BY ROSIE ROLLIN.

I had to start somewhere. How hard could it be? Just pack up what you need, load it on a horse and set out. That is sort of how I got started on what I like to call "short-long riding." When this bug hit me, and trail riding became my main focus after several years of horse showing, I had a pretty good idea where I wanted to ride. For several years I had kept my horse at a wonderful place called Long Lane Farm in Maryland, in the shadow of Sugarloaf mountain. A beautiful spot where horses enjoyed large and lush pastures and lots of equine friends. Horses are herd animals and love the company of their own kind. My paint gelding, Zorro, was fat and happy there. I was working full time so riding on the weekends was a passion. There was a group of us who met there every weekend, come snow, cold, wind or rain. We loved our trail rides and good company. Our early rides were mostly 4-5 hours, and we had some very young children along on their ponies. Then, as the kids got older and we got bolder, our rides became all day affairs complete with a fun lunch stop where we would build a small fire and roast hotdogs (tube steaks) and make hot chocolate. Those were the days my friend!

Our horses all tied well, and we sat around the fire, sometimes in the snow, and enjoyed the moment, thoroughly. I guess that is when the idea first started growing in my head that I should take a camping trip on my horse. One of the wonderful places that we had to ride was the historic C & O Canal that runs along the Potomac River from Washington DC to Cumberland MD, a distance of 185 miles. It has been described as the longest bridle path in the USA! The C & O Canal was not yet a National Park, but Justice Wm. Douglas of the US Supreme Court was an avid hiker, and he was a force behind getting it to be a National Park. What happened in 1971. I believe that the cost to the government was two million dollars for 6000 acres, a long and skinny piece of land, that had been a significant part of US history. The canal was begun in 1828 and was completed in 1850. The need was for a waterway where coal could be transported to DC from the West Virginia mines. The river itself would have been too dangerous, not to mention impassable in many places (have you ever seen Great Falls?). This canal is a treasure. It is 185 miles long and has a 3000-foot-long tunnel, 75 locks to raise and lower barges, 7 dams and 11 aqueducts. Now, when I rode it, it was in disrepair, having been abandoned in 1924 by a severe flood (and the railroad). But the lives lived along that route for 74 years left a lasting legacy along its way. A lot of the workers who built it were Irish immigrants who seem to have Roman stone masons in their blood because the tunnel and the aqueducts are works of art in stone. Rome had left its influence in the UK many centuries before and stone aqueducts were common there.

It came to pass that in 1965, I took that long sought after camping trip on the towpath of the C&O Canal. Because they say that there is safety in numbers, I talked two friends into making this trip of a lifetime with me. Pat was a gal coworker and Doug a 17-year-old high school student. We all three boarded our horses at the same farm and rode the trails on weekends. We did plan and prepare a little. We made our own saddlebags since this was back in the day way before these things were used by anyone but western movies and/or real cowboys out west! We made them from army surplus knap sacks, sewing one on each side of a piece of leather. Perfect. We also carried two tents, a sleeping mat, a rain slicker, and a wool army blanket that we had made into a sleeping bag. We were psyched and ready!

Since our starting point was near the Monocacy Aqueduct (at mile marker42.2 or 42.2 miles from Washington DC and 142.3 miles from Cumberland MD) on the canal, that is where we picked up the towpath, riding north toward Cumberland, MD. Each aqueduct is unique and the Monocacy one is the longest, having 7 arches over the Monocacy River. This was the first of 10 aqueducts that we would cross or go around!

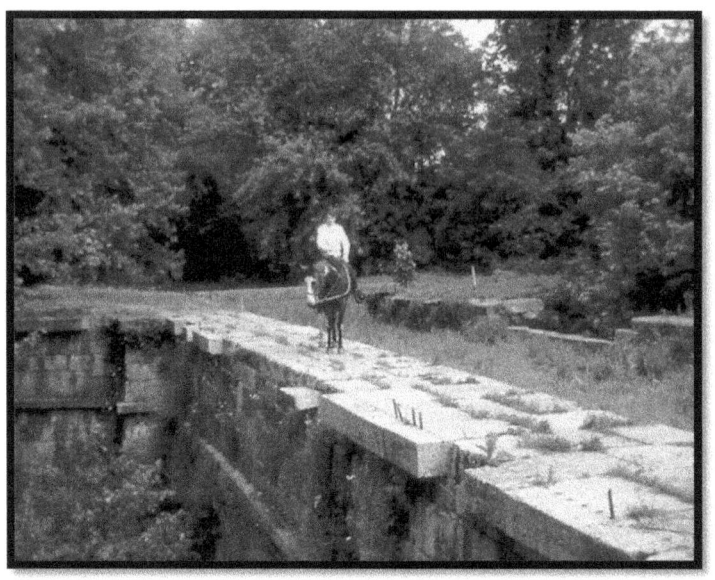

Rosie On Zorro On An Aqueduct

Some are in disrepair having been washed out in floods. Some you can ride right across the now grassy middle (where canal water once sat) and some you cross on the stone walls where the mules towing the barges walked. We were familiar with the Monocacy aqueduct having ridden across it many times on our weekend rides. We rode the walls because you can see daylight down along the grassy bottom and the river below that! Yikes. We would not want to fall through! An aqueduct had to be built across each creek that flowed into the Potomac river, to let the canal barges pass above and across the creeks. The C&O Canal was a magnificent engineering feat, having been built mostly with only hand tools and manual labor, and its structures like the aqueducts and locks stood the test of time fairly well. There were 75 lift locks to raise and lower the barges from sea level in Washington DC to 605 feet in the mountains at Cumberland Maryland. There were 7 dams built along the Potomac River which enabled the canal to be filled with water. It was a life unto itself with not only canal boat families, but mule drivers and lock tender.

The locks were operated 24 hours a day! Coal was moved from the mountains to the sea on this waterway. Talk about job opportunity!

We picked up the grassy towpath, now shaded by big, overhanging trees after crossing the Monocacy Aqueduct and began our northward trek toward Cumberland, Maryland. When the canal was in operation, there were no shade trees between the towpath and the canal. It had to be clear for the mules and the tow ropes that pulled the barges along the waterway. I was grateful for the shady path on this late June day. Each of our horses was carrying about 200 lbs with rider and gear. I was on my faithful paint gelding, Zorro. Pat was riding her chestnut gelding, Shane and Doug was riding his bay gelding, Stony. We had divided up the supplies so that we were all about equally loaded. This was my first pack trip and being only self-taught, I must say that I learned a lot on this adventure! We had seen our first snake before we even reached the canal.

We had to ride about 3 miles to reach the towpath. We then saw a big black snake on the towpath. We found that we could only walk with the bulky loads, so when we stopped for lunch, a little north of Point Of

Rocks, we all made our packs more secure so that we could jog/trot a bit. Some of our tie rings got ripped off here and there, but nothing drastic happened. Our spirits picked up a lot when we found that we could move on a little faster now. Walking, walking, walking becomes very tedious and tends to make knees and butts sore, but a short little canter/lope and jogging keeps the muscles working and limber. We soon encountered our second aqueduct over Catoctin Creek. Unlike the Monocacy aqueduct, it is too dangerous to cross, so we had to detour around it along the railroad track which at this point runs parallel to the canal. We arrived at Weaverton, at mile 58.3 where the PATC (Potomac Appalachian Trail Club) has a nice campsite. We got there about 6:30pm and proceeded to set up camp, take care of horses and prepare supper. It started to rain, lightly, but the trees gave us shelter. I made some repairs to our saddlebags and tie rings. We fed and watered horses and pitched our two small tents. Pat and I would share one tent and Doug would have the other one and most of our supplies. We dined in splendor on ham sandwiches, apples, cookies, and hot tea. We built a fire every evening for cooking and warmth. We carried a small, metal grill frame that we could set up over the fire for a cooking surface.

It worked well. We tied our horses to trees. High lines and picket lines were not in vogue at that time. Leave No Trace camping has now changed how we tie horses ... so they cannot chew on the trees! Our horses, Zorro, Shane and Stony all tied very well. We crawled into our tents at 9:30pm. I slept pretty well on my little air mattress and wrapped up in my wool army blanket. I got a bit chilly towards morning, a problem that increased as we made our way northwest.

We got up about 6am, fed and watered horses and ate our breakfast of cereal and hot tea. It was a beautiful morning. The Potomac River is very wide here and we were camped under a huge elm tree that shaded us. We had many daddy longlegs and ants here! Few night sounds but nice birds chirping at us in the morning. We saddled up and got away at 10:10am. It was taking us a while to get packed up, but we would get faster and better at it every day. We had started at mile marker 42.2 and this morning we rode past historic Harper's Ferry, where the famous John Brown attack on the Union arsenal took place just before the Civil War. The town and the bridges are quite picturesque from the towpath on the Maryland side of the river. Harper's Ferry is at mile marker 60.7. We had come about 19 miles. Here the train left us. It crosses the river, and we were glad not to have it beside us now. Today, a Sunday, we met some Boy Scout troops, fishermen and families out for a picnic. We stopped for lunch about noon and ate jerky and water. The horses had not settled into drinking from the river each time we offered them water, but they would get better at this too. They seemed to think that we would be turning for home soon. In fact, each morning for the entire trip, the horses would turn for home at the start of each day! We watched some people water skiing on the river while we ate our lunch. About every 10 to 20 miles, we came to a "hiker-biker overniter" campsite which we used sometimes. We were careful not to camp too close to these campsites which had a picnic table, an outhouse, a cleared area for tents and a water hydrant that could be hand pumped. We did not want to pollute the nice camp spots with horse manure! Another Leave No Trace goal. All of us and the horses seemed to be in good spirits. We headed on towards Antietam and came to a nice spot with lots of picnickers and a fine, cold well. We filled all our canteens. A local man who was fishing directed us to a small, country grocery store. We rode up to the store and stocked up on canned spaghetti, Vienna sausage, canned peaches, pears, cheese, hot dogs, and rolls. We met a nice man at the store, and he directed us to place where we could camp and keep our horses overnight. We rode on to this place, ½ mile above "Miller's Saw Mill" and two miles south of Sharpsburg (you have to know that the Union called it Antietam and the south called it Sharpsburg!).

The man we sought was Howard Churchley and he was an angel for sure! He gave us enough grain for two good feedings, fresh eggs, and directions to a great camp spot on the towpath. He apologized that he could not put us up at his farm because he has 50 horses turned out in his pastures! Yikes. He was so very nice and would not take a penny for any of the goodies he gave us! We made camp about 5:30pm, having ridden about 13 miles today. We had a good camp complete with an outhouse and a good place to swim in the river! We had brought bathing suits for that. We took care of horses, set up camp and then enjoyed a feast of fresh scrambled eggs, hot dogs, rolls and hot tea. Canned peaches for dessert. Delicious. We did our dishes, took a swim, and did some laundry in the river. The horses all drank well and after our swim we led them to a good grazing spot that Mr. Churchley had told us about and let them eat for about 30 minutes. We secured our horses for the night and sat around our campfire, drank hot tea, and played at the ukelele that we had brought along. Into the tents at 10pm.

    I slept well until about 4 am and then I got chilly. I wore legatards and a sweatshirt to sleep, but just the one blanket is not enough. Pat's horse, Shane, got caught in his rope and fell … I cut him loose … he was OK. Doug was great with the fires, and he would get one going in the chilly mornings while Pat and I lay wrapped in our blankets! We ate the rest of the fresh eggs, jerky, oatmeal, and hot tea. We fed and watered horses and they were doing well. We passed Lock 40, at mile marker 79.4, and Taylor's Landing. Above here the canal is really authentic, being water filled and having no trees between the canal and the towpath. We rode along in silence feeling the history. We reached dam # 4 at mile marker 84.4 at 3 pm. Next to the dam is a covered bridge structure over the canal, perhaps a lock house from which things could be loaded on and off the barges from above? The bugs were pretty bad along here and the sweat bees were driving the horses nuts. Here, the canal enters the river via a lock, and we were forced to follow a rocky, narrow, grassy footpath along the edge of a now very deep river! The canal averaged only about a 6-foot depth; the river, being damned here was about 25 feet deep! We arrived at a little marina with a small store. The man here let us put our horses in his son's little pasture, a beautiful meadow with good grass and a stream through it. How nice was that? We bought some grain at the store and camped in the meadow. Our horses were glad to get loose and they rolled and rolled. they sloshed in the stream and enjoyed the freedom. We ate spaghetti and hot dogs with cheese for supper. Whenever we stopped at a store, we bought and ate popsicles and soft drinks, something we could not carry with us. The nice son loaned us his fishing boat and we scouted up the river to study the towpath that we would have to travel. the path is very narrow for about ¼ mile until we can pick up the towpath again. The boat was delightful! This Mr. Wolford was very nice. We retired at 9:30 pm in the meadow, now knowing what we would face tomorrow.

We arose about 6 am, packed up quickly and got an early start at 8:30am.

The first part of the trail was very narrow, rocky, and rather treacherous! No canal here, so no towpath as such. The canal boats took to the river here. After a little less than a mile of this poor footpath, we passed lock 41 (at mile 88.9) where the canal began again. We picked up the towpath and soon passed locks 42 and 43. We stopped often for pictures. We saw many houses along this area known as Falling Waters. A little girl on a bicycle rode along with us awhile and told us that "Indians had fought on those walls!" We saw some stone abutment and an old bridge. We came to a rather bad washout area just before lunch. It was difficult for the horses to get across, but they were game. We found a nice place for lunch a couple of miles south of Williamsport. We had to eat up our canned goods before buying more, so we enjoyed a can a piece of Vienna sausages and canned pears. The trick was to stay one meal ahead of the next town!

After lunch we rode up the main street of Williamsport after immortalizing the Conococheague aqueduct on film. We bought food for the saddlebags and several popsicles! Back to the towpath with our goodies. The path is good but sooty in this industrial area. Many rocky places along here. We rode a long time this afternoon. We passed a quarry and crossed several pastures with many gates to open. We saw lots of Boy Scouts on bikes today!

We were looking for dam # 5 as a possible camping area for tonight but we were terribly disappointed when we came to the dam; no approach to the river for the horses and a narrow footbridge to cross. More bad news; rocks and another washout area. We had crossed the narrow bridge and rocks but had to turn around and go back across them and locate another way. We rode on and on. The horses were tired and thirsty. We finally found a place to stop: Four locks at miles 108.6-108.9. There really are four locks here in just 0.3 of a mile! Beautiful. We had a nice picnic area, a picnic table, and a place for a campfire. No grazing though and muddy swimming. We had a good supper of lasagna, fruit cocktail and hot tea. It was soon dark, and we had to water horses and get our dishes done. To bed.

Our fifth day was another beautiful day. We had been very lucky. The sun was not yet very warm however and our laundry had not dried! I hate to have to pack the extra water weight! We were all getting used to sleeping on the ground because we did not get up until 7 am and we all slept well. We had apricot nectar for breakfast with cinnamon buns and hot tea. The horses appeared to have dropped some weight from our 20-mile ride yesterday. And there was not much grass for them here either. We must buy some grain for them at a nearby farm. We allowed them to graze as we walked along the towpath. We were so slow packing that I had some doubt about us reaching Hancock, 15 miles up the towpath. We got away about 10 am and this day turned out to be hot and humid. There was a pump just a short distance north and we stopped to fill our canteens. That well was sort of hidden off the towpath. We rode on and passed a couple of unmarked ruins, McCoy's Ferry, and Fort Frederick? The towpath here seemed rather endless as we passed through Big Pool State Park. There was a nice breeze although we were out of sight of the Potomac River along here. There were many farms and fields. We saw woodchucks and flushed some quail.

We came to the Licking Creek Aqueduct at mile 116. We rode on past a body of water on our right; this was Little Pool, soon followed by locks 51 and 52 at mile marker 122.9. About 4 miles south of Hancock we passed a nice hiker-biker camp spot that we may try to hit on our back south. It was too early to stop today! We had a town to meet! We had only eaten jerky, cheese, and water for our lunch today and were looking forward to a grocery store. We needed grain for the horses and rode smack into Angle's Feed & Lumber Co. What a piece of luck. We went in and purchased 10 lbs of oats for each horse. We shopped at a small grocery on Main St. and restocked our supplies.

After riding out of Hancock and back to the towpath, we began looking for a place to camp. We did not come to any camping or watering areas at all! We finally turned down a little side path towards the river, as we needed to water the horses. It turned out to not be a very good spot. Knee deep mud and lots of what we thought might be snake holes in the ground! Yikes. It was also quite buggy here. Just not a good spot in any way. We all agreed to ride on into the evening. We stopped long enough to feed the horses some oats and we ate our supper of steak sandwiches on rolls and canned fruit. We remounted at 6:30pm and rode on into the beautiful evening air. We were all in great spirits and so were our horses after their oats. We hit a hiker-biker about 9:30pm and made camp. There was no water for the horses here, but we pitched our tents and hit the sack.

This was day 6. We got up and had toasted buns, hot tea, and orange juice.

We were somewhere near dam # 6, about mile marker 131. We packed up and left rather swiftly in search of water for the horses. Dam # 6 is not much of a dam anymore. It was not holding back any water anyway. The day was cloudy and cool with rain threatening. This was the first bad weather day we had had. We were all kind of dirty from lack of a good swimming spot last evening and we were all carrying wet &/or dirty clothes. We passed lock 55 and found really good watering for the horses. They drank well. We crossed Sideling Hill Aqueduct at mile 136.6. This was our 7th aqueduct. We took pictures at every one of them! We found a good camping place at lock 57 (mile marker 139.2) with an outhouse, but we did not stop, having only come about 7 miles today. We always make a note about the camp spots as we may hit some on the way back. We were still searching for our "perfect campsite." We crossed Fifteen Mile Creek Aqueduct, which was in pretty good repair, about noon. This was an A-1 camping spot, but it was full of campers! There were some park maintenance men working and they told us that the next hiker-biker was at lock 62, about 12 miles up the towpath. In August of 1938, the US government took complete possession of the C&O Canal and although it would not become a National Park until 1971, the Park Service was making necessary repairs in some places. Our short day was wearing on. We stopped at the aqueduct for about 2 hours to eat our lunch and to give the horses a rest break. We had Vienna sausages, jerky and pears. We ate on someone's front porch and let the horses graze in the yard. It was raining rather hard at this point, so the porch was nice. We almost decided to camp here despite the crowds because it did have outhouses, a pump and good beach access, but we did not like all the children around the horses, nor the fact that we were on private property! So, we pushed onward.

We arrived at lock 62 at mile 154.2, having come about 22 miles today. This, as it turned out, was our "perfect" camp spot! We have passed about 8 locks today. This must have been a place of slow passage for the barges with so many locks along this stretch. I learned though that it only took about 10 minutes to get a barge in and out of a lock but if you had to pass through 4 or 5 of them fairly close together, a back up might have been expected. I would have loved seeing the canal in its heyday. The trees and wildflowers along the canal are quite varied. We saw another wild turkey with her babies. She hid the chicks off the trail and then diverted our attention to keep her babies safe. We had seen a lot of tortoises. They sun themselves on the logs and downed trees in the swampy parts of the canal and dive into the water as we rode past them. Hundreds of them! It is very beautiful along here in the mountains. It does not get much better than this for fun. It had started to clear up as we reached lock 62 and the sun burst out. It was still rather cool, making it pleasant for the horses. We unpacked, watered the horses at the pump, fed them oats and made camp. We swam, washed, did laundry, and enjoyed ourselves at this great spot.

The river was chilly and delightful with a good rocky bottom (instead of mud). Nice. When we got out, we were moving quickly because it was cold. We cooked ourselves a divine supper: one of our freezedried dinners of sliced beef and gravy. I made some mashed potatoes to go with it and they were fabulous. We had "turblocken," a glucose-freezedried block, for dessert. I was fantasizing about cheesecake for some reason.

Our whole supper was superb. We did our dishes at the pump and grazed the horses for 30 minutes before securing them for the night. The sky was lovely and the Big Dipper magnificent. Later in the night we saw the milky way. Doug's horse stepped on a nail today and he is a little worried. We would contact a vet when we get to PawPaw or Oldtown.

We hit the sack about 11 pm and just laid there listening to the frogs and crickets.

We had been cold in the night, but the morning was beautiful, and we hung our laundry out first thing. The sun dried everything rather quickly. We ate soup and tea for breakfast. That seemed odd, but it warmed us. I missed our fruit juice. I sat on a bridge over a lock and watched the bees working at the chicory. The horses were munching grass noisily. The laundry dried. I watched a little chipmunk scamper about. The sky was a thrilling blue with a few small clouds. I gathered my laundry and did my dishes. We remained at this nice spot until afternoon. We had chili and beef for lunch. Absolutely delicious fare.

We began slowly packing up after our filling and satisfying lunch. We delighted in the sunny, crisp day itself. We got off about 2 pm and hit a couple of peculiar locks: 63 1/3 and 64 2/3. Odd. Then, we crossed a long, wooden bridge. The canal, filled with vegetation here, is very narrow and a sheer rock wall rises to our left. Just around the next bend was one of the objects of our anticipation, the PawPaw tunnel! It is over 3000 feet long and curves slightly so that we could not see the daylight at the other end! It had taken 8 years to build this passage. It is a work of art being totally brick lined. The towpath and the waterway pass through this 21-foot-wide tunnel. It has remained in remarkably good condition for over 140 years. The towpath is very narrow but there was a substantial railing between the path and the canal. Parts of the path have been repaired with boards, so it was a bit surprising to hear my horse's clip clop on wood at times! We started through with Zorro in the lead. I got out my flashlight about ½ way through and was shocked to see that parts of the opposite wall were caved in. The brickwork was awesome. When I could see daylight at the other end, it seemed so close … but it seemed an age before I was once again in the bright sunlight. Shane and Stony had followed Zorro closely and when we exited the tunnel, Shane walked quickly away putting as much distance between himself and that scary trail! We were pretty proud of ourselves for having ridden through this famous tunnel. We rode up to a road and to a nearby store for groceries. I bought 30 lbs of grain for $1.86. All the people at the stores are very nice to us.

We rode back to the towpath and moved toward an unknown goal. We were searching for another hiker-biker camp spot but were not going to ride too long today. We crossed the Town Creek Aqueduct and rode alongside a large farm, found a place to water the horses and kept on riding. As we reached lock 68 (mile164.8), a man came out of his house right beside the towpath. He was holding a guest book for us to sign! He had gotten signatures from almost every traveler since 1935. His name was Isaac Long. We signed and felt honored to do so. There was a hiker-biker on the other side of the canal here. Mr. Long showed us the way to get over to it. He stayed and visited with us and was absolutely delightful. He told us some very interesting news: the Oldtown, Maryland Annual Fishing Rodeo is tomorrow (a Saturday). We would be very lucky to get to see this special event. He also told us about National Geographic articles that he has helped with. He is the secretary of the Oldtown Sportsman Club which puts on the rodeo. He told us about several interesting travelers that he has met over the years. He told us about a 77-year-old woman from Ohio who called Supreme Court Justice Douglas a "lousy hiker." She carried nothing but a jacket, a sweater and an umbrella and walked the towpath from Cumberland to Washington in 9.5 days, at a leisurely pace! She had killed a puff adder and scared off a wildcat along the path! I would loved to have met her!

Mr. Long showed us the way to lead our horses to the river for water. It brought us down to the river across from the mouth of the South Branch of the Potomac River, where a railroad bridge crosses the South Branch. The towpath now picks up the North Branch of the Potomac River. He left us telling us not to miss the rodeo tomorrow and that we may have trouble riding past 1700 children on the towpath! He also gave us some welcome information about what is ahead (besides the rodeo): that this was the last hiker-biker up this way but that the next good place to camp would be at lock 73. There would be a spring there for watering and the lockhouse has a porch. Our horses could graze on the lock. Good info.

We let the horses graze out back of Mr. Long's house until 10 pm and then we prepared to hit the sack. The bull frogs are marvelous, the sky is lovely, the air is cool and tomorrow promised to be another perfect day. We had enjoyed minute steak sandwiches, applesauce, cookies, and hot tea for supper. We felt satisfied. Mr. Long delighted us with his chatter about the people he had met.

The next day was sunny and bright. It had been a cold night and we found that it was hard to get moving on these cold mornings. We got up about 8 am. I guessed that Mr. Long was already up at the rodeo. It is only 1.5 miles up the towpath from our camp. After a delicious breakfast of toasted rolls with jelly and hot tea, we began to pack up. A park ranger drove up in his scout. He told us that it would be too risky to ride the horses past the crowds at the rodeo. He kindly offered to drive us up to the Oldtown store, bring us back with our groceries and grain, and then take us to the rodeo to watch and eat. How nice was that? We went with him and found the jeep a rather bumpy ride on the towpath compared to our horses! Rangers Parkinson and Robertson were very nice to us. Ranger Robertson is new here and is just learning all the different flora. He is a schoolteacher in Gaithersburg, MD. They both know Ranger Bill Clark from down at White's Ferry way on the canal/river, whom we know from our frequent rides in that area. Small world.

That fishing rodeo was a fantastic event! Kids of all sizes, shapes and ages competing for over 100 prizes. I only saw 2 unhappy children all day: one was unhappy because it was time to go home, and the other little girl had a fishhook in her leg! The rest of the 1700 folks were all jovial and were enjoying the day. It was a perfect day and a man in town told us that only once in 17 years had they had rain for the rodeo. I took a lot of pictures of the kids fishing. We walked uptown, after eating some delicious 15 cent hamburgers, and we saw the House of History. It seemed that George Washington kept some headquarters there. Pat called home and I wrote some postcards. We walked slowly back to our camp and horses to begin packing. We started off at 4 pm. The crowds had thinned to just a handful and we rode through without any difficulty. What a fun adventure this was. We began searching for an old lock that Mr. Long had told us about. It had a spring nearby. We got to lock 73 at 6:45 pm and found that it was not the one that we were searching for, so we turned around and rode back to lock 72 (at mile 174.4), where I found the spring! Yea. We had to pitch camp right on the lock. We put our gear on the porch of the lock house. Nice. We cooked a fine supper of beefaroni and had canned pineapple and cookies for dessert. Hot tea always tasted good. I still was craving a piece of cheesecake. We washed and watered the horses at the spring and then sat on the lock for a while and chatted about our day's adventure. It was getting much colder and after donning many layers of clothes, we turned in about 11 pm. The night was very cold, and I did not sleep well at all.

We had decided to get an early start, so Doug got us up before 6 am. Wow, it was cold! Wearing our blankets for warmth, we ate toasted rolls with jelly and hot tea for breakfast, sitting close to our fire. We packed everything to go and then made a big decision. We would not spend another night this far north! So, we stowed our packs and gear in the bushes (out of sight) and rode "naked," that is, without our packs, which enabled us to travel much faster. We took only our cameras and hit the trail at a lope, heading for our northernmost goal, the Evitt's Creek Aqueduct (at mile 180.7). We would not ride into Cumberland MD, a very busy town. We flew up the towpath feeling free and successful. As we got closer to Cumberland, we saw more and more houses, noisy trains, and road noise. I was not happy with all the trains near the canal. In fact, I disliked that the trains had moved in and wiped out this glorious period in our history. I am more of a non-mechanized person. The day warmed in the bright sunlight, and we got to the aqueduct, took the appropriate pictures proving that we had made our northern goal, and headed back to lock 72 at a fast gait. The horses loved it … we were finally heading in the right direction … home!

We ate our lunch (Vienna sausage and cheese) at lock 72 and put our packs back on. Three men rode up on horses! They were returning to Cumberland after having ridden down to Little Orleans, about a 45-mile ride! These were the first riders that we had seen. We hit the towpath south about 1 pm. The day got warmer, and our horses have picked up speed now heading toward home. We would make better time now! We reached Mr. Long's at 3:30 pm and set up camp. I was looking forward to visiting with Mr. Long again. I wanted to look more closely at his collection of letters and autographs. He introduced us to many fine people at the rodeo. He told us that 343 fish had been caught at the rodeo, including one trout! Mr. Long showed us where the spring fed canal spills over a dam, a divine spot for a shower! We all took advantage of it. The cold water was refreshing, and we really felt squeaky clean after that. We had beef chunks and steaks with mashed potatoes (instant) and fruit for dessert. Yummy.

After a nice visit with the Longs, at their home, we had hot tea and turblocken. We retired about 11 pm. A wonderful day.

We arose about 7:30 am after our first warm night, which was very nice. I slept like a rock, warm and cozy. We had a rather blah breakfast of toasted rolls with nothing on them and hot tea. We slowly packed. I liked this spot more and more. I wandered around and snapped some more pictures. The Longs are really darling, good people. We mounted up and rode off about 9:45 am, heading towards PawPaw.

We made such good time (since the horses were stepping out nicely) that we decided not to waste a stop for lunch and to push right on to the store at PawPaw. We bought more groceries, goodies, and more grain at the feed store. We managed to pack it all in our saddlebags and headed into the PawPaw tunnel. It was not nearly so scary or thrilling this second time through. I liked the dark, cool, and clammy long tunnel. The walls above the path in the tunnel have been repaired. It is brick, stone, and mortar. Little trickles of water seep down onto the path. The two-board railing is solid and held up by iron posts (some original). The canal had water in it through the tunnel, but it must have come just from leakage from above because the canal is dry with lush green grasses and black willow trees at each end of the tunnel. The wall opposite the path had caved in places which was a shame because this lovely structure was like nothing I had ever seen in the whole US. This canal must be preserved. It is a much more fantastic part of our nation's history than many tourist attractions across our country. One can feel the canal, its bustling activity, the quaint lock houses, huge warehouses and loading docks, the working locks, spillways, and the aqueducts. I learned that the tunnel itself is 3140 feet long and it took 14 years to build, at 14 feet/day. Our government purchased the canal (6000 acres) in 1938. It became a National Monument in 1960 and began to reflect some improvements by the park service. It became a National Park in 1971. It had originally cost $11 million to build. It is a National treasure in my mind!

We reached our "perfect" campsite about 2:30 pm ... old lock 62 and a hiker-biker. It felt like home to us! We set up camp, took care of the horses and did laundry. We had found a better place to water the horses than at the pump this time by. The sun up on the lock was so warm and bright that we were able to wash and dry everything. A delightful breeze helped too. A pair of my dainties blew into the canal and Doug fished them out with a hook and line! We ate sloppy joe sandwiches and applesauce for supper. We went swimming a second time as the river water was just marvelous. We swam out to the middle where there was a rocky, shallow island. Great fun. We snacked on tuna fish and cookies. To our tents at 11 pm. It was a pleasant night for sleeping.

We did not get up until 8:15 am on this Day 11 of our trip. We were seasoned campers now and enjoyed the night and morning. We had hot soup, cinnamon buns, and hot tea for breakfast. We all hated to leave this beautiful camp. We dragged our feet while toying with the idea of remaining here an extra day, to play and relax. In the end, we packed up and rode out at 11:20 am. My watch had stopped at 6 pm yesterday and I had been hoping that time would stop all together. The mountains were so pretty, and this was a perfect spot-on earth. There was a nice breeze this day which is always nice to keep the bugs away. We slowly passed the locks in descending order along the 7-mile bottom. Doug found a lovely spot for lunch through a big, yummy field and down by the river. We ate peanut butter and jelly sandwiches. The views up and down the Potomac River were out of this world here. We were between locks 59 and 60 somewhere. Mile 147. Shortly after lunch, Ranger Parkinson drove up behind us on his way to Hancock. He wanted to know if we had called our folks since he had seen us at Oldtown! He was checking up on us! He was very nice, kind and concerned, good qualities in a Ranger.

We rode on to Little Orleans at mile 140.9 and stopped at the store there for a few items. We rode back to Mr. Stevenson's leased land and camped way down by the river. We cleared a spot for the horses' way back in the woods so as not to ruin the mowed lawn (which some other riders had done!). The mosquitos here were as big as airplanes according to a fisherman we met! We did some laundry and went swimming. Wonderful weather. We had spaghetti and meatballs for supper and fruit cocktail, cookies, and hot tea for dessert. The mosquitos drove us to bed about 10 pm.

The next day (12) we wanted to get an early start as we had a long way to ride to get to Hancock (16 miles away). We had very little grain for the horses last night and this morning. It was showering lightly when we got up, so it took a little longer to pack up. We did have our toasted rolls with jelly and hot tea for breakfast though. We got off about 9:30 am under a now cloudy sky.

The sun was in and out all day with no rain. We had a leisurely lunch about 12:30 pm (peanut butter and jelly sandwiches) after riding 9 miles. I spotted several big, fat wild turkey today and a lot of chipmunks, turtles, and wild ducklings. We passed an enormous cave on the other side of the canal. We rode into Hancock about 3:30 pm and shopped. We bought grain again at Angle's Feed & Lumber and Stony got a tetanus shot from a local vet, Dr. Shives. Stony never was sore or lame but we felt better that we got him treated! We mounted up and rode south, laden down with groceries and grain. Yea! We hit the Little Pool hiker-biker about 5 pm. We made camp and washed the horses in the river. We cooked a marvelous supper of minute steaks, mashed potatoes, and peaches. Cookies and tea. I was stuffed. We have been eating well! We talked for a long time this evening and watched the sky fade into night. A slit of moon was visible. We did not swim or do laundry here since we were located just below Hancock and the river is dirty. It did feel good on our feet though. A nice breeze came up and the night was perfect. We retired about 10:30 pm and slept well.

Rosie on Zorro
in the Potomac River

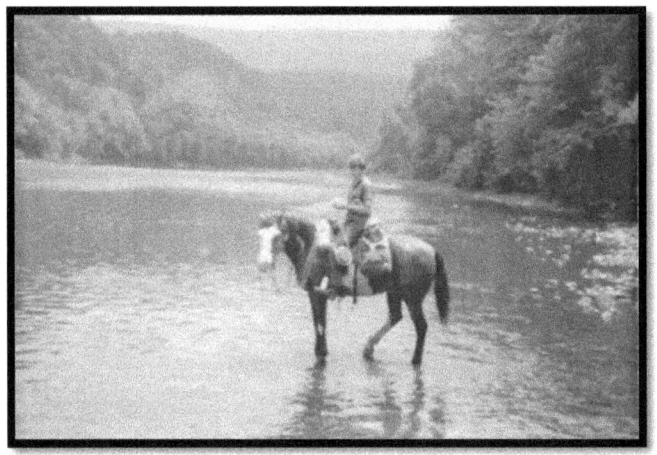

We were at mile marker 120. This was Day 13 and we had ridden about 190 miles in all. We were tickled with how good we felt and how good our horses looked and behaved! It was July 1st. Time was passing too quickly. I was dreaming about cheesecake again! My mosquito bites kept reminding me that we were roughing it on the trail...and the daddy longlegs were a friendly bunch! I got up first this morning, at 7:30 am. I crawled out of the tent and found it to be rather chilly, but I did not have to wrap up in my blanket. I just moved swiftly! I got a raging fire going and Doug got up to see if I was burning the place to the ground! We had hot chocolate and sweet buns for breakfast. Yummy. This was another pretty campsite, like most of them had been. It had lots of big, old shade trees that cover the area like a canopy.

Lots of young trees coming along as replacements when the big ones fall. There must have been some strong wind here recently because we had seen several fallen trees in this area.

This hiker-biker has the usual picnic table, covered trash can, fire ring, water pump, an outhouse and good access to the river. We hit the trail at 9:45 am. We rode just from Little Pool to Big Pool (mile 113) and stopped for lunch. The day was beautiful, the sun warm but not hot, and the towpath looked like a long shady tunnel. We enjoyed tunafish and PBJ sandwiches and the ever-present cookies! We got moving again at 12:45 pm, but a halt had to be called after we passed through a gate and Pat's saddlebag was torn from top to bottom! Whoa! Repairs were made and we continued on to Four Locks, arriving there at 2:30 pm, making for a very easy day of only 13 miles.

We washed clothes and ourselves as the water was delightful. We found a place to go in off a pier to avoid the mud! We were all in great spirits, almost punchy with all the food we had been devouring. For our supper we had chow mein and noodles for something different. Pears, cookies, fig bars, ice water and peppermint patties for dessert. No cheesecake.

We grazed the horses a bit and chatted gaily until bedtime. We had met two boys (twins I thought) on horses today. They were riding from Williamsport to Cumberland. They seemed to know horses well and took good care of theirs, but some horse riders/campers had left Mr. Stevenson's place a mess. We hoped that Ranger Parkinson did not think that we had left that mess! We later met Ranger Bell on the towpath and told him to please let Ranger Parkinson know that we had cleaned up the mess that some other folks had left at Mr. Stevenson's. We were actually trying to practice Leave No Trace camping although that had not come into fashion in 1965!

July 2, a Friday. We got up at 6:30 am and enjoyed cinnamon rolls and hot chocolate for breakfast. It was chilly this morning. The river had a deep cloud of mist hanging over it which made it seem even colder. We did not carry a thermometer, so only if we found ice on the water would we have a clue about the temperature! I was wearing my blanket around that morning. We had a long day of riding ahead of us, so we got right to our packing. I took more pictures, and we rode out at 8:45 am. We made a good time that morning despite the rocky trail that was hard going. We reached Williamsport (10 miles) by noon and did our shopping. We bought groceries and film. After leaving the town, we rode on a while before stopping for lunch. It was the same spot where we had stopped on our ride north. The trail had a couple of washouts along here and a bulldozer has cut around them. Our lunch of tuna and PBJ sandwiches was rather dull as we were still kind of full of cinnamon twists from Williamsport! We had hostess sweet buns for dessert!

We rode on towards Mr. Wolford's place. The trail never seemed dull here as there were too many exciting trees, wildflowers and black raspberries begging to be picked. We made it to Mr. Wolford's unscathed by the narrow section of trail sandwiched between the river and the rock wall. A rocky carpet beneath the horses' feet! Mr. Wolford was delighted to have us back! We got the same deal as before. The horses were so glad to be let loose in the pasture to roll and graze freely. We cleaned up a little and then went down to have supper at Mr. Wolford's little snack bar. He was quite nice once we got to know him! I did our cooking in his shop ... cheeseburgers and "steamers" (all ground beef sandwiches). I stuffed myself again on popsicles. We sat on the pier in the evening and felt it get chilly for a short while, but then it warmed up again. Weird. We visited with a man who lives up on the hill, over the water, with his wife and two boys. They live here all year round. He showed us around one of the fancy houseboats he had helped build. Then, he took us for a ride up the river in his speedboat! Wow, was that great? It was dark and the running lights looked so cool against the spray from the boat. His 12-year-old son was at the helm! We retired shortly after that thrilling ride. We were camped in the field with our horses, and they were a little annoying during the night, trying to eat all our bags around the tents! Doug had to get up and chase Zorro away!

Day 15: We got up at 6:30 am. I listened to bobwhites and a nearby rooster.

The night had turned out to be quite warm and I had not slept very well due to the horses running past us. I thought we were going to be trampled ... the ground shook when they ran past! Rascals. We did not make a fire this morning. We had a small amount of apricot nectar, bread, and jelly. I missed something hot to drink. This was the first morning that we had skipped a fire. We packed up and got away at 8:30 am. I hated to leave this little oasis.

We made good time all day. The horses were fit and ready to go. We passed Dam # 4 (mile 84.4) today. The canal has been drained and some trees cut out of it along here. I wondered if they were getting ready to fill and use it. We stopped along the towpath for lunch, about 10-12 miles south of Mr. Wolford's. We had PBJ sandwiches and sweet rolls again. We also ate the last 3 pieces of our beef jerky. We watered the horses and then got prepared for inclement weather as it began thundering fiercely with some lightening! We no sooner got back in the saddle at 1 pm and had to put our slickers on. It was a heavy but brief shower, and nothing got soaked except Doug's hair! The sun came out about 2 pm and it was nice the rest of the day. We pulled into our camp spot about 2 miles south of lock 39, at 2:45 pm. We had made excellent time on our return south! We had stayed at this spot on our way north. It was OK but it lacked a picnic table which we missed. It also lacked water to drink. Fortunately, since this was a small campsite, and this was a Saturday night, we were lucky that no one else was camped here! We set up camp and went swimming. We also washed-out hair! I had felt very clean at all times on this trip. The river was cold after the rain, and we did not stay in the water for very long. We had chicken & rice stew, fruit cocktail and cookies for supper. All yummy after a good day in the saddle.

About 7:30 pm while we were waiting on our freeze-dried dinners to soak up water, an elderly man and woman came striding into our camp. He was a very interesting person, a doctor in Shepherdstown, WV who often walks the towpath. He told us that he has covered over 75 miles of it just doing occasional walks. He was very impressed (or jealous) of our adventure when we told him that we had been out for 15 days! It did not seem possible to me either! We were all having a marvelous time. Our horses were in grand shape. Our diet was good, and we all felt healthy and happy. This gentleman, Dr. Wanger, had hiked with Justice Douglas. He was very interested in Mr. Long (at Oldtown) and recommended a very good book about the canal. By Sutherland. I made a note about that. Dr. Wanger is very active in the medical world and was well acquainted with NIH (National Institutes of Health) where Pat and I worked. The lady with him was Miss Noleen and she too was very interesting having taught school all over the country, wherever she felt like going! She was originally from Iowa. She was presently taking some courses at American University. Dr. Wanger told us that he hikes up at Harper's Ferry a lot. After they left, we finished preparing our supper, ate and retired about 10 pm.

Sunday July 4th! Independence Day! Yea! We got up about 7 am and found several early fishing parties about on the river. There were lots of children and we had to keep a close eye on the horses. We ate toast with jelly and tea. It was a little chilly and our fire felt good. We packed up and got away at 9:20 am. We rode first to Howard Churchley's place to see about getting more grain, but no one was home. I saw one of his appaloosa stallions! Wow, what a beauty! We were sorry not to see Mr. Churchley and he would have been tickled to see how good our horses looked now. We rode on to Antietam and were pleased to find the store there open on Sunday, and on this holiday! We stocked up on bread. We did not have any luck finding any grain. We rode on and stopped for lunch at the same little picnic area where we had stopped before. There was a lot of activity on the river and at the summer cottages and camps. Every now and then we heard a firecracker! It was the 4th of July after all! The river was dreadfully low. We noticed a difference from just two weeks ago. At Dam # 3, which is 2 miles above Harper's Ferry, we were able to walk clear across the river on the rocks! No water was coming over the dam at all. Two weeks ago, we had seen water pouring over it!

We reached Weaverton PATC camp about 3:30pm and luckily, no one else was there. Yea. We tied the horses and I set out on foot to go look for grain, while Pat and Doug set up camp. I walked up to Weaverton and asked some people who had chickens if they had any corn, they would sell me. The Sullivans were a little leary of me at first ... I was trail dusty, tired, hot and was carrying an empty gunny sack! Once I introduced myself and told them who I was and what I was doing (riding the towpath), they were quite friendly. Mr. Sullivan works on the trains and travels alongside the towpath everyday. He claimed that he had seen us up at Evitt's Creek Aqueduct! They were very interested in our adventure and asked me many questions. They, too, like me, were amazed that we had been out for 16 days. It did not seem nearly that long, nor long enough! I bought 10 lbs of corn from them and walked back to camp feeling successful and happy. Our camp was all set up and we gathered wood and began preparing supper. The horses were happy to see me with a sack of corn!

Just before we began eating, a Boy Scout troop walked in! They were from Pennsylvania and were hiking a portion of the Appalachian Trail, which joins the C & O Canal here. They were all very nice boys and reflect a good scoutmaster! They took right to the river, even though it was low, dirty, and rather smelly. They all felt better after a couple of hours in the water! We did not swim here. We went on with our gourmet supper of chicken stew, mashed potatoes, and creamed corn. Canned peaches and ginger snaps for dessert. Yummy. We had passed a couple of obstructions on the towpath today; trees that were downed by the storm yesterday. It apparently hit this area much harder than where we were. Whole trees had been blown down across the towpath and we were lucky to be able to find ways around them. A little dog had followed us from Wolford's place, and we hoped that he found his way home. He quit following us after a while.

This was our last camp! Sad to think that this adventure would end tomorrow. It had been all fun. We turned in about 10 pm. The Boy Scouts returned from an evening walk to Harper's Ferry about 10:30pm and they turned in too. A nice group of boys.

We kind of slept in until 7:30-8 am on this last day of our trip. The Boy Scouts used the fire first and gathered lots more wood. Nice. They ate beans, ravioli, Vienna sausages and potatoes! Not exactly my kind of breakfast food. Our group had more traditional fare of scrambled eggs, toast with jelly and hot tea. Yummy. We packed slowly because no one really wanted to go. We finally got off at 10:50 am! We rode slowly south and stopped for lunch just before Point Of Rocks. We ate PBJ sandwiches, tuna sandwiches and ginger snap cookies. We set out toward home.

It began to cloud up and we had to break out our slickers for only the 2nd time on this trip. The rain came down rather hard but the tall tree canopy above us broke it up a bit. I did not get wet or uncomfortable at all and my big slicker covered me and my pack very well. We all looked very colorful with our bright yellow coats against the dark horses and green trees. Visibility was poor and the river was quite rough. We still had good daylight left so instead of heading to the farm at Noland's Ferry, we rode on to the Monocacy Aqueduct and crossed it at 4:30 pm on day 17. Yea. This was where we started this ride and thought it nice to return to our starting point. We stopped in at some neighbor's place to shout our success and those folks complimented us on how great our horses looked. We rode on to the farm where our parents were waiting for us. At least they hoped that we would arrive there today! This was in the days before cell phones and constant communication, so plans were a little iffy. It was a grand homecoming, and our horses were delighted I'm sure to be back home. Our folks had brought us fried chicken and CHEESECAKE that we had all been craving! Thus ended a 17-day adventure on horseback.

THE TEVIS

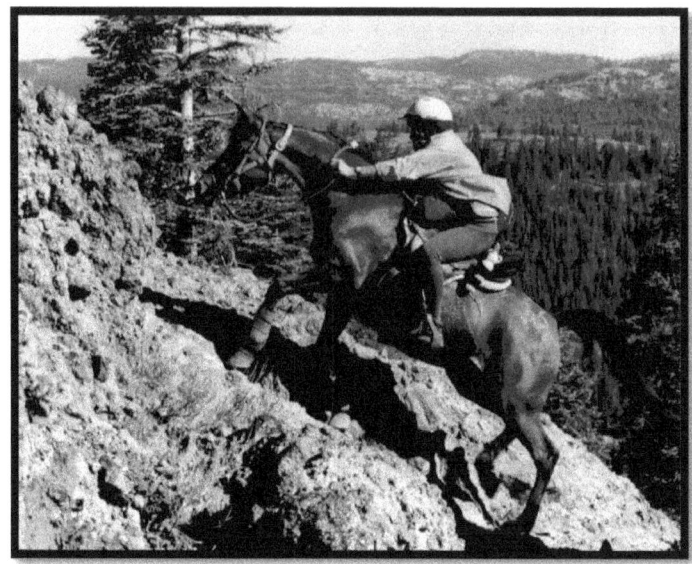

Rosie on Blu at Cougar Rock in California
(courtesy of Hughes Photography)

It is officially called The Western States Trail Ride. It is affectionately known simply as the "Tevis." The first place trophy is named after Lloyd Tevis, president of Wells Fargo & Co. from 1872 to 1892. He went to California in 1849 and no doubt Mr. Tevis, his horses, coaches, and express riders traveled parts or all of what would become the historical Western States Trail through the difficult Sierra Nevada range and down to the foothills. This is a 100 mile- one day ride ... not for the fainthearted! The Donner party got stuck in these mountains in 1846 and only 49 of 91 emigrants made it out of the mountains ... a story that crossed my mind a few times while I was riding the trail! In 1955 a man named Wendell Robie started the Western States 100 Mile-One Day Ride. His name is synonymous with the ride. He completed the ride 13 times, winning it 4 times. This year, 1998, was the 44th running of the Tevis and all who ride it are eternally grateful to those, living and dead, who have worked tirelessly to run this event. My girlfriend, Dixie, and I went out to California to ride the Tevis this year. Dixie had completed the ride in 1973 and earned one of the coveted silver buckles for finishing. She wanted to give it another go on this her 25th anniversary. I wanted to give it a first time try. This is my account of the ride Dixie, and I left Virginia on Sunday July 26th. We were hauling our horses, my Blu, and her Zack, to ride the Tevis trail. We were accompanied by our dogs, Ginger, and Queenie. We did consider ourselves certifiable, hauling a horse 6000 miles to ride 100 miles, but we were out for a good time and a total western adventure with plenty of fun stops along the way. We reached California on August 1st after some fun adventures, including a stop-to-wade at Lake Tahoe immediately upon crossing into California! We also stopped at the base of the Squaw Valley ski area so that Dixie could enjoy a moment of nostalgia ... this was where the ride began when she rode it in 1973. It was pretty humbling to look up at the snow-capped mountains and think that in 7 days we would be riding up that hill! We spent the next week letting our horses rest at a friends' place near Auburn, CA. These dear friends have paid me good money not to reveal their names or location ... it became a popular spot as the ride drew near! It was a "resort" complete with swimming pool, air-conditioned house (very important during this El Nino year when the temperature soared to 107 degrees), gorgeous stable, a private pasture for our horses, top quality hay, and just about anything a person could want or need!

These are really, really nice folks if you get my drift! On Aug. 4 and 5 Dixie and I took our horses out to the end of the 100-mile trail, in Auburn, at the fairgrounds, to ride the last 4 miles in the daylight, since we would be riding this part in the dark on ride day.

If you show your horse the trail, he will remember it the next time you do it. Besides, 4 miles from the end of the trail is the famous No Hands Bridge ... and we wanted to get pictures of ourselves on it! It is a 3 arched bridge built in 1912 over the American River. this is the only bridge that has stood the test of time and flood in that canyon! It is an old railroad crossing high above the river and it is on the historic register. I felt thrilled to take my horse across it! Dixie had ridden across it, under the full moon, in 1973, but now we are asked (required) to get off and lead across it. I took some good pictures of us on that structure!

On Thursday Aug. 6th we hauled our horses up to Robie Park, near Lake Tahoe, where the ride now starts, at 7000 feet. It sure felt good to get up to the cooler temperatures in the mountains. We got our horses checked in on Fri. and attended the pre-ride supper and meeting that evening. Lots of our Virginia friends were there and we had a good time with them. To bed late Fri. night, after preparing all of our tack, food, and clothing, to dream of the trail and control our fears!

Up at 3:30am to prepare for the 100-mile day. We felt that we were as ready as we could be. Our goal was not to race, but to ride sensibly and hopefully complete. Just to put it in perspective, almost 7000 people have attempted this ride and less than 2000 have completed. Those statistics are not near as good as the Donner party! Everyone who finishes is awarded a silver buckle ... well earned. There were 220 horses starting the ride this year and Dixie and I got into place about 4:30 am for the 5:00 am start. We thought that we were someplace in the middle of the pack, but it is almost impossible to tell where you are in that dusty crowd, in the dark. The ride starts promptly, and I got my first thrill at that! The dust raised by just one horse can be choking and the dust from 220 horses was like something from a Spielberg movie! I wore my bandana pulled up over my nose like a highway robber! By the time we had covered the first 10 miles it was getting light out. We reached the base of Squaw Valley and began the 2500 foot climb up to the snow fields. The trail here is mostly a dirt/gravel road to the top where we were surprised to see a couple of the ride veterinarians watching the horses trot by. This was right at the Watson Monument with Squaw Peak to our left and Granite Chief Peak on our right. The Watson stone cairn is a tribute to Robert Watson who helped immensely in finding the old California trail in 1929. We were at 8700 feet now, the highest point on the ride. It was here where Dixie turned to me and said "Well, it's all downhill from here." Because we were at the highest point now and the trail ends in Auburn at 1200 feet, it would seem that it would be mostly downhill ... not so ... this is what makes this ride so difficult and challenging ... there is a total of 18,000 feet of up (climb) and 23,000 feet of down! It takes a tough horse to do this! It has been said that "this is not a ride for snivelers." Keep that in mind. ... I was on a high as we crossed the ridge known as Lyon Ridge. That is about 10 miles of narrow trail with lots of little rock outcrops to challenge your horse. There are several creeks/bogs along this stretch where the horses like to stop for a sip of water and that backs up the single file line at times. This is definitely a no passing zone! I was snapping pictures and changing film all the while. The scenery was magnificent (understatement!!). At 23 miles we reached the infamous Cougar Rock where a photographer waits to take pictures of each rider. It may be your last living picture! The rock is a big outcrop that you must go up and over. Maybe 50 feet up with a turn near the top. It lends a breathtaking backdrop for photos! I was told 2 rules to follow in going over Cougar Rock ... don't stop and keep kicking! That turned out to be very good advice and both Dixie and I had excellent climbs and have envious photos to prove it! If you have a Cougar Rock photo, any endurance rider will know that you have done the Tevis! I was really enjoying this whole thing now! In fact, I had been enjoying the whole trail since the start. After Cougar we rode across Red Star Ridge through some beautiful pine forests with gorgeous views across vast canyons ... must have been really frightening to the early settlers and miners. We reached the first vet check at 36 miles, at Robinson Flat by about 11:15 am. So, it had taken us 6 and 3/4 hours to do more than 1/3 of the trail ... piece of cake ... we had 24 hours to complete it. I felt that we were on a good schedule to complete. The day was perfect ... about 80 degrees with low humidity ... the best weather they'd had for this ride in the 44-year history! We were fortunate indeed. Some years it is 120 degrees in the canyons! Yikes. We got through the vet check in good order, but we lost a little time giving our horses an extra 15 minutes to fuel up (eat grain and hay). They still had a long way to go today. We left that stop at 12:30pm and enjoyed a long, easy downhill segment on gravel road that wound down a mountain in a series of easy turns. Just before Dusty Corners, a teddy bear seated on a lawnchair and sporting a Western States hat pointed the way! Our horses were happy to reach this next stop where they inhaled top quality alfalfa hay while waiting to be checked out by the vets. We were treated to watermelon, cookies, fudge, and apples. Keep in mind that it is the horse's well being that is monitored and watched, not the rider ... we are on our own! We carried snacks and fluids (water and sports drink) and were happy to get the free goodies at the stops! We had now done 46 miles and were looking and feeling great. Just before Dusty Corners I had dismounted in a creek to throw water on my horse and I slipped on the wet rocks and fell completely into the creek. That felt good actually, but I feared that my camera may have suffered a fatal blow and I spent the next few miles trying to dry it off. I poured water out of the battery chamber and used my bandana to dry the inside. I loaded new film and peered through a foggy viewfinder for the next few hours! I was really going to be disappointed if my pictures did not turn out! At 50 miles we passed a marker that told of the historical significance of this portion of the Western States Trail. This portion is on the National Register of Historic Places in the US, just as is the No Hands Bridge at 96 miles. We dropped down into a canyon, enjoyed a cool dip in the north fork of the American river and then crossed the "Swinging Bridge" which really does swing! It wasn't that scary though and a photographer took our picture on the bridge. Up a steep series of switchbacks, climbing yet another 1726 feet, brought us into the stop at 56 miles, called Deadwood. Our horses tanked up on water here before we pushed on through El Dorado Creek canyon, a drop of 2665 feet followed by a climb of 1830 feet! This one about finished off my horse! It was endless ... but beautiful! At least it was still daylight! We finally reached Michigan Bluff at 63 miles at about 8pm. Hummm ... it was getting dark! Our horses were tired and hungry, but they munched a good bit of good hay here and they passed the vet check looking good. Dixie and I felt pretty good, and I was still elated about how pretty the trail is! We saw the TevSweep riders getting their night riding gear ready to ride drag behind the last horses and realized that we were about the last horses now! It was a little reassuring to know that emergency assistance would be following us now that it was dark. We did a fairly fast 6 miles into the vet check at Foresthill. We were met here by our faithful, hardworking, enthusiastic, long-suffering, reliable and encouraging pit crew who had all our necessary supplies here for us. At this point I made a trip to the outhouse and got lost in the dark trying to find my horse! When we were reunited, I got my nightlights tied on and made sure I had working flashlights. Because it took us so long to get through the vet check here, we decided that it was necessary to give our very tired horses an extra 30 minutes to rest and eat. This turned out to be a cardinal error, but I am not sure that we could have gone on had the horses not eaten and rested. We left Foresthill at 10 pm with the full moon rising! It was a little hairy riding down the main drag of Foresthill on a Saturday night. We had to go just a few blocks along the busy paved road before turning down a sidestreet that led us to the trail. At this point the trail headed downhill through a tree shrouded canyon and the moonlight did not help us in here ... we had to use our flashlights some to follow the switchback trail. Our horses were still quite hungry and after we had gone about 8 miles, we stopped on a switchback to feed them a few fat pellets that we had carried for just such a need. We were into the American river canyon now and the trail was getting more lit from the moon. At times the trail was down quite close to the river and then, without even realizing that we had climbed a bit, we were on a sort of bluff trail high above the river. Much to my horse's disappointment, there is absolutely nothing to nibble on along this 18-mile stretch. I felt that this is too long a stretch this late in the day! Our horses were getting increasingly tired and hungry, and we began to worry about them. Dixie began to lament about this being far different and much more difficult than she remembered from 1973. In fact, this part of the trail was different than it had been in 1973. An easier canyon had been used then. We were hoping that the drag riders would catch up to us and we could tell them that we were going to stop because it was now obvious that we were not going to make it to the next stop in the time allowed. I was disappointed but still found the trail beautiful. The full moon was reflected in the river below like a million-watt bulb! Dixie began singing a ditty about the next stop (Francisco's) ... "Where oh where has Franciscos gone, oh where oh where can it be ..." The trail seemed endless and yes, we had to chastise ourselves for being snivelers! I announced that I would never try this ride again! I can't believe I said that! I got off and led my horse for about an hour. She was pooped. I still felt pretty good all things considered, but it was kind of disappointing to now realize that we would not finish and collect a silver buckle. We could see some lights a long way ahead and it appeared that the lights were leaving, and we got worried about that. We kept wondering where those drag riders were too. We finally rode into Francisco's at 4:00am having ridden 86 miles in 20 and 1/4 hours of riding time. I was proud of every mile!

The ride personel had not left Franciscos and were there with hay and blankets for the horses, a chair, and some blankets for me! They were glad to see us and gave us a warm welcome. There had been a problem with the drag riders that had been following us ... one of their horses had kicked the other in the nose and broke the nose which made a medical emergency because the horse was having difficulty breathing! A vet and a rescue had to be made for them, so as it turned out, no drag riders were behind us! After a 1-hour rest during which our horses consumed about a ton of hay, we had to lead our horses up a 3.5-mile hill to meet our faithful pit crew and trailer. As we climbed the hill, the sun came up while the full moon was still up. It was really a pretty morning. Being out on the trail this long does afford one the opportunity to see 5 celestial events! Sunrise-sunset-moonrise-another sunrise and moonset! Cool. We hauled our horses back to the lovely resort that they had come to know and love, and they seemed tired and hungry but ok ... we were sure glad for that. Whew. After we had taken care of our horses, we showered and fell into bed for a 3-hour nap from 9 am-12 pm. Then, we drove over to the fairgrounds to partake of the awards dinner and to watch the awards. This year 121 horses finished, which is the best rate ever. One of our friend's from VA finished 25th on her first try at this trail. Excellent. I sure would have liked to have finished, but I am most proud of my little horse and the job she did. She is not a good uphill horse, and I had my doubts about all the climbs, but we did all the hard parts, and I loved every inch of the trail. It is awesome. In spite of my 4 am announcement about never riding it again, by 5 pm that same day I was saying "next time ..." and I will give it another go sometime. There is a quotation about the 19th century travelers that sums it up: "What they had done, what they had seen, heard, felt, feared ... the places, the sounds. the colors. the cold. the darkness, the beauty ... til they died, this stream of memory would set them apart ..." I will treasure my memories about the 1998 Tevis as long as I live!

ROCKY MOUNTAIN RIDE

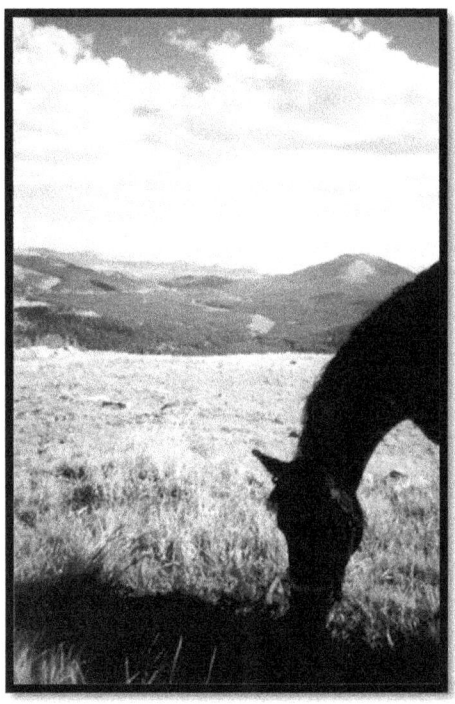

Blu on Boreas Pass in Colorado

The Rocky Mountains are in the western United States. They run north to south and pass through several states, like Montana, Wyoming, Colorado, Arizona, and others. Way back in the year 1873, an Englishwoman, named Isabella Bird, came to the western US to spend some time in the Rockies. She seemed to always have health problems when she was at home in England, so her doctor told her to try taking a trip for better health. Isabella was to become known as an explorer-writer and adventurer after taking many trips for her health!

She arrived in the mountains of Colorado by train in the month of September when the Colorado Rockies are the most beautiful with the aspen trees turning golden before winter arrives. Isabella was a very good horsewoman and she loved to travel about by horse. She was happiest when seeing the country from the back of a horse. In Colorado, she found a little cabin to rent up in the mountains and she stayed there for a month, riding about the country on a rented horse. She helped local folks round up their cattle and met several mountain families who lived a tough existence in these mountains.

After a while of seeing the same scenery, Isabella got an idea to take a trip around Colorado to see more of the country. Colorado was not yet a State. She met with Mr. Byers, the founder and editor of The Rocky Mountain News (a newspaper) and went over maps with him. They came up with a rough plan for Isabella, traveling by horseback, to travel a big, circular route to see more places and meet more people. It turned out to be a trip of about 600 miles which she did in about 30 days. What Isabella did not know yet was that October in the Rockies is the start of the winter snows! At times she found herself trying to urge her horse through snow that was chest deep and in temperatures below zero! In 1873 there were no Holiday Inns nearby. She would not think about stopping or giving up on her travel plans. She was on her own. She stayed at ranches, at boarding houses when she was near a town or in abandoned cabins (some without a roof). Her first priority, always, was the wellbeing of her horse. She had rented this little, bay horse, named Birdie, from a nice family and she intended to return the animal in fine shape. Isabella and Birdie became a great team. She described the pony like this: "She is the queen of ponies and is very gentle. She is always cheerful and hungry, never tired, looks intelligently at everything, and her legs are like rocks. She is quite a companion, and bathing her back, sponging her nostrils, and seeing her fed after my day's ride, is always my first care." At times, when the trail was very rough, Isabella took off her socks and pulled them on Birdie's feet so the horse would not get sore feet! She always made sure to take care of Birdie at night before she took care of her own needs. That is the sign of a great horsewoman!

Isabella wanted to ride all the way west to Breckenridge Pass where she would cross the continental divide at 12,000 feet elevation! She needed to do this before the snow got any deeper because the pass would become closed then. Her trail was not like the roads and interstate highways of today. She was often riding little deer trails and following creeks shown on old maps. She did accomplish her full circle ride and returned to the cabin where she had begun, after returning a healthy and fit Birdie to a grateful family.

Now, my story begins. I had read about Isabella Bird's ride in Colorado, and I got an idea to take my little, bay pony and re-ride some parts of her trail. What a fun idea! First, I had to study the map and after reading her account of her trip, I had to piece together her ride from landmarks, known ranches, towns that remained, creeks, mountain passes and one sketch that Isabella had done of Breckenridge Pass. It was a fun undertaking.

I am an endurance rider. That is, I ride my horse in 50-to-100-mile races on trails all over the country. Trying to re-ride Isabella's 600-mile route did not intimidate me at all. Isabella was riding between 30 and 50 miles a day on her trip. I would not be riding her entire loop of 600 miles, but I would try to ride portions of the trails where she rode. Because it is now more than 100 years later, parts of her trail are now interstate highways and large cities, making it impossible for me to ride there. So, I looked for parts that remained forest and country. Lots of Colorado is now part of our wonderful National Forest system and some remains as open country where cattle graze during the summer months, which is perfect for a horse rider. I could haul my horse in the trailer to an area where Isabella rode and then saddle up and ride in her hoofprints! I discovered that Breckenridge Pass, where Isabella rode up to the continental divide, the highest point on her ride, is now called Boreas Pass. It looks just like it did in her day! Gorgeous. She made a sketch as she approached it, and I snapped a picture with my camera! I saddled my little "Birdie" horse, named Blu, and we headed up to the pass on a dirt road. At the top I encountered some tourists who asked who I was, and when I told them the story of Isabella and her 1873 ride, they were fascinated and interested enough to write down the name of her book which I told them about. After enjoying the views, taking lots of pictures, allowing Blu to graze a bit, and just feeling the same high that Isabella experienced up there, I turned Blu around and rode back down the mountain. A wonderful day for me.

Since Tarryall Creek is still on today's maps, I drove over to an area of National Forest where I could camp that night and then ride another portion of Isabella's trail the next day. I enjoyed seeing Blu drink from Tarryall Creek, the same one that Birdie had sipped. I followed the creek west and then looked for a pass over which Isabella must have come from the east. Blu carried me up, up and up and we broke out of the timber and the view was breathtaking. No wonder Isabella loved this ride she did! She rode across what is today the Pike National Forest and, on another trip, I rode right through the ranch where Isabella and Birdie has passed. They spent a night at the Parker Ranch where Isabella enjoyed a rare, comfy bed and hearty meal with Mr. Parker's daughter, while Birdie had a nice warm place in a barn and good feed. At least they had great comfort on that night! Just being near where she had passed, brought a smile to my face. I did this in September and October, which was about the same time that Isabella had been there. I, too, suffered in the 20-degree night air. I did not encounter chest deep snow, but only a few flurries at times.

Isabella and I share another love (the first being horses) which is hot tea. We both enjoy a cup of hot tea at the beginning and end of the day.

She carefully carried tea with her, as did I. At one point on her trip, she left Birdie at a livery and took a train up to see a gorgeous, high mountain lake, called Green Lake. Because that entire road is now paved, I drove my truck up to see and photograph that same lake. I try to use my imagination to see it just as she did. I blocked out the paved road and the power lines! In her day, it was a big mining area, and the train was used to carry in workers and supplies, as well as to carry out the ore.

Isabella preferred to ride alone, which I can understand. When you are on a horse that you totally enjoy and ride through beautiful country, you really don't want anything to interrupt your tranquility. However, had I been around when Isabella started out on her ride, I might have asked her if I could join her! What fun that trip must have been despite the hardships. If a person worries about where to sleep, where to get food, cold temperatures, and the dangers of the outdoors, he should not think about taking this kind of ride. Isabella did get lost one night and finally found a house at midnight where she was glad to stop. I have ridden my horse all night and you do get tired, if not a bit anxious.

She kept a diary about her adventures and wrote letters home to her sister in England. These letters later became a book about her adventures in Colorado. I am always appreciative of folks who keep written records of their adventures so that a reader can relive the adventure. Isabella left Colorado in December 1873, never to return. Later, she often wrote of the Colorado rockies and their majestic beauty.

Because I can travel to the western US, I can continue to enjoy the mountains every year. Thank you Isabella Bird.

NIGHT OF THE CLOUDY MOON

Rosie on Cloudy Moon
(courtesy of Hughes Photography)

The call came on the 4th of July ... a message left on an answering machine. I had already decided that I just could not take my horse to California, what with gas at $2.00/gal! I was just about resigned to fly out to California and pit crew for friends this year. I just had to take some part in the Tevis experience ... I could not get enough of it! So, I fielded the message and was granted a minor miracle: a friend had an extra horse and would generously and graciously lend it to me for my 3rd Tevis try! I could not believe my good fortune.

So, I packed up my saddle, helmet, shoes, and riding tights and flew to California 4 days before the 46th Tevis 100 mile-one day ride.

The next morning, I met "Cloudy", a beautiful gray Arab/warmblood mare who was my kind of horse ... laid back, cool under any circumstance and that special kind who takes care of herself and her rider. On Wed., 3 days before the Tevis, I took the mare out for a 10-mile ride. We hit it off. We hauled our 3 horses up to Robie Park, where the Tevis trail begins, on Fri. morning, one day before the ride. We set up camp and got the horses checked in. Now, since Cloudy was my friend's spare horse, I breathed a sigh of relief when her primary horse vetted through just fine. Whew. So, I was really in the ride! Let the jitters begin!

There is an excitement about the Tevis, an electricity in the air and the Robie Park setting is perfect for the pre-ride dinner and ride briefing. We had hit the vendors for the Y2K Tevis shirts (with a picture of the swinging bridge on the front). I find that I get little sleep the night before any ride, but my friends had graciously offered me a comfy cot and sleeping bag in their tent, so I actually got a few hours of good sleep under the full moon.

Up at 3;30AM. It was unusually warm this year, probably 55-60 degrees. Dressing yourself and your horse in the dark (well, by moonlight anyway) is always a task where experience counts ... what you hope for is that everything is on in the right direction and that it stays on for a long time! My two friends and I mounted up at 4:30 AM after downing a sports breakfast drink and a hardboiled egg. We were ready. I think due to a film crew from Japan, here to record this Tevis, the start was delayed 15 minutes so there would be more light. We hit the trail at 5:15 AM!

I love this ride and every inch of this historic and scenic trail through the Sierra Nevadas in the hoofprints of the Donner party and the Pony Express!

The 3 of us were just going to "mosey on down to Auburn" as was suggested at the pre-ride briefing last year! Yeah, right. With 259 horses starting all at once, it's more like a cavalry charge for the first 5 miles! I had a moment of angst when Cloudy stumbled behind when her rear brush boots got stuck to each other by the velcro straps! Yikes ... she almost went down! I hopped off to readjust the boots only taking seconds. Our 2 mares and one gelding stuck pretty close to each other, but it's definitely everyone for themselves in those first few miles. And don't forget your facemask, the only thing between your mouth and the dust! We made it to Squaw Valley at mile 10 and reconnoitered, took stock, and found ourselves very upbeat and feeling great.

These 3 horses we were riding had been bred and raised by my friends' late Mother ... and a fine job she had done! All 3 of them were 12 yrs old, strong, and willing but sane and pleasant. I felt totally safe which makes a ride truly fun. Nevertheless, I had dressed in my usual bright colors in case a helicopter had to come looking for me! Last year a very experienced Tevis rider had to be airlifted from the Squaw Valley area after a bad spill!

We zipped across Lyon Ridge with only 1 of our 12 hooved legs caught in a rock V ... "Go forward. Go forward" I yelled, and my friend's mare extricated herself from the trap. Whew. No damage. We made our way through the rocks along the ridge and through the pine forests occasionally spotting the flapping helicopter above that was filming a Japanese journalist trying to conquer her first Tevis. Her's was a sobering experience, as her leased horse was ill and pulled at the first vet check (36 miles). I wondered if the filming would continue ...

We chose to go around the infamous Cougar Rock as 2 of us have pictures of us on that landmark taken in 1998. Across Elephants Trunk and along Red Star Ridge ... we were trotting along at a good pace when a passing rider said to me "I think you lost a shoe"!! Yikes. We pulled up and I set a world record (for me) in slapping an Easy Boot (a kind of spare tire) on that naked hind hoof! Jeez. We rode on into Robinson Flat at 36 miles where we were greeted by our intrepid crew of about 15 people ... it seemed like a thousand helping hands! Something was seriously wrong with me ... I was having leg cramps! While our "best ever" pitcrew (they had already crewed 3 others in our group through this check) took care of Cloudy's rear shoe and then set her to eating (the horses are really hungry now), I downed 2 cans of Ensure, a Boost and a quart of Gatorade. That took care of the muscle cramps. That was a first for me. O.K., time for confessions ... I am usually in fit-as-a-fiddle riding shape, but this year I had been very busy building my new house and had not gotten in much riding. I had only been on a horse 7 times all year! Of course, one of those rides had been the 50-mile Old Dominion (half-a-ride to the purists) in June. My body was rebelling to this insult. Lucky for me, Cloudy was a very comfy and kind ride!

We said farewell to our crew, as we would not see them for a long time, and onward we rode ... down to Dusty Corners where a stuffed teddy bear in a lawn chair points the way. We went on past Dusty Corners and into a new and different vet check, called Pacific Slab Mine, at 51 miles. After this brief check, we started into the first canyon. We decided to dismount and jog down which certainly was going to bring memorable quad pain tomorrow! But it was a nice break for our horses not to have to carry us down. We crossed the picturesque swinging bridge at the bottom of this canyon. The next canyon is the very long and tough Eldorado which seems endless, both down and back up. We still felt that we were making good time as we reached the Michigan Bluff vet check at 63 miles. Cloudy was getting tired and I was getting worried about her, but on we rode.

As we were chugging along through Volcano canyon a rider caught up to us and told us that he had helped rescue a rider who was clinging to a tree after her horse mis-negotiated a switchback near the canyon edge and fell over the cliff!! WHAT??!! What happened to the horse I asked ... no one knew. The girl rider was pulled back up and onto the trail, but the horse could not be seen or heard! It could have fallen hundreds of feet! Dear God ... that sobered us up.

The reality of it is that every horse and rider is at risk on this trail.

We rode on into the Foresthill vet check and I sort of felt like a gold medal Olympian walking up the road lined on both sides by onlookers cheering every horse and rider! What a rush! Here we were at 69 miles, and it was dusk. Our wonderful crew was there with food for horses and riders. I was starting to fade a bit and the sandwich that I was encouraged to eat, and the cup-o-soup were very comforting. Cloudy was looking just a wee tad off, but since no one could put a finger on it, she was cleared to go. Whew. This is a 1 hour stop, so by the time we left here it was dark. We rode down the main drag of Foresthill avoiding cars and looking for our turn down into the American river canyon. We would be on that trail along the river for the next 18 miles ... a long stretch that far into a race! It had taken me 6 hours to do this stretch in 1998 which resulted in my "overtime" pull from the ride that year. We did it in 3 hours and it did seem endless again. At this point, the full moon is supposed to be lighting the way ... well, this year, the moon was hiding behind thick clouds and the trail was like the inside of your pocket! We had very few moments of moonlight that night. It's fun riding along and chatting with passing riders. A group of riders, obviously a bunch of locals, wanted to pass us as our lights were bothering them ... they know this trail and can make better time in the dark letting their horses head for home. The vet check at Francisco's (at 86 miles) was busy and crowded. About half the finishers will cross the finish line within 2 hours of the deadline and with horses slowing down in the dark and/or getting tired, the trail gets crowded in those last 14 miles. We headed on toward the river crossing at Poverty Bar and decided that my friends should pull their bright lights hooked to the horse's breastplate up to keep them from getting electocuted on the crossing in the knee-deep water!

The water level here is lowered by a dam just for the ride each year ... it would normally be too deep for a horse to cross. The next 5 miles into Lower Rock Quarry vet check seemed the longest stretch all day! I was really getting tired and sad to say, I was whining a bit! I apologized to my friends ... I was lamenting about not being in very good shape this year and told them that I was in better building shape than riding shape ... and that I could have stopped anywhere on this trail and built us a log cabin but riding 100 miles was starting to look beyond my grasp. Lucky for me that after Lower Rock Quarry I knew the trail and started to brighten up at the prospect of actually finishing this ride! We crossed the No Hands Bridge 4 miles out and headed for the finish line. When we came up out of the woods and into the bright lights at mile zero and saw our crew there cheering us on, I was exhilarated ... not to mention totally exhausted and starting to feel a bit ill. Lucky for me, Lynn trotted Cloudy out for me both at the mile zero check and at the finish in McCann

Stadium. Yes, that really is the name of the stadium. I think I went into some kind of fog at this point. I was half sick for a bit and Carey got me some crackers to eat which made me feel better. Our crew members and Cloudy's owners saw to her comfort and all 3 of the horses were fine.

At this point, about 5:30AM Sunday I sort of lost track of the details, but we returned to my hosts estate, and I showered and fell into bed ... I think. We were planning to attend the award ceremony at 3PM that afternoon. We skipped the 1PM lunch.

The awards ceremony is interesting and exciting ... for the finishers. I had been there twice before as a non-finisher, so this was going to be special for me.

First, they bring the top 10 finishers (horses) into the stage area so people can see what a horse who finishes this race in 15 hours looks like. To get any completion in an endurance race, the horse must be "fit to continue" judged by a panel of veterinarians and the top 10 horses do look incredible! They look like they could head down the trail some more! It is impressive to see them.

The winner is the first to finish and that horse and rider win the Tevis cup. Perhaps the most prestigeous and coveted award, however, is the Haggin Cup awarded to the horse judged to be in the very best condition and that often is a horse who has finished in 3rd to 8th place. There is a lot of applause for the Tevis and Haggin Cup winners ... and rightly so!

After the top ten awards, the junior rider awards and the 1000-mile buckle winners are honored, all the finishers are brought to the stage to walk across and pick up the Western States Trail Ride 100 Mile buckle. Out of 259 starters, we finished 99, 100 and 101 out of 129 finishers. To finish is to win is the motto for endurance riding and everyone who completes is awarded a silver buckle. Some competitors have over 20 buckles! I am humbled. However, I asked for the microphone when I crossed the stage and gave my little speech: "I came all the way out here from West Virginia to do this ride and proved that the 3rd time really is the charm ... for this was my 3rd try! I want to thank some wonderful folks for lending me such a great horse for this ride and our "best ever" and devoted pit crew who were there for us. I would also like to take full responsibility for the cloudy moon last night, for the beautiful mare I rode was named Cloudy Moon! Now, as some of you may know, the Western States Ride mentored our Old Dominion Ride held in VA each June. I would like to challenge all you western weenies to come try for one of our coveted buckles! Thank you." I walked off the stage to the sounds of laughter and cheers! All in all, it was a really fun and fulfilling experience and I am forever indebted to all the nice folks who made it possible for me. I thank you.

Oh, as a postscript: at the awards ceremony we got word that the horse who fell into the canyon was found and he was ok! It was a miracle ... he had only fallen about 70 feet and came to rest on the edge of a cliff! Some men went out to search for him and he was found 24 hours after his fall. The men were able to make a trail to lead him back up to the trail at the top. The horse was relatively unscathed, and it was a happy ending ... thank goodness!

ONE OF MY BEST RIDES

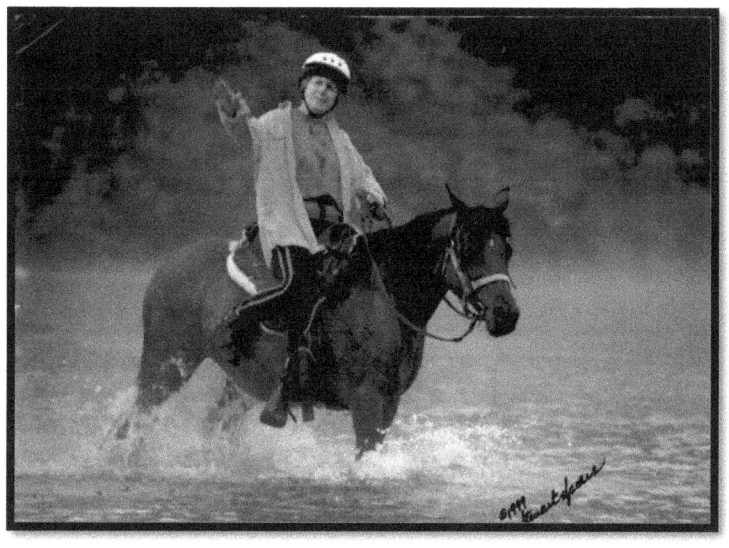

Rosie on Blu crossing the Shenandoah River in Virginia (courtesy of Genie Stewart-Spears Photography)

It was a stroke of good fortune indeed that I even started the OD 100 this year (2001), thanks to my friend, Lynn Golemon, who calmly came to my trailer and said, "Need any help getting ready?" No, I said, I think I've got it under control (having put my clothes on).

Lynn then said, "Rosie, it's 4:45 am." WHAT? YIKES! How could that be??? Obviously, I had looked at my watch wrong. The start was at 5AM! Lucky Lynn was there to help and that we are like minutemen when it comes to saddling a horse! We carried my saddle, pad, martingale, and bridle to my stall and had my dancing, prancing mare dressed and out to the ring by 4:57. I checked in with Henry, the official timer, mounted up, went into the ring and BAM, the trail was "open for competition". Whew. Darn, and I rather like some breakfast and having some time to warm up my horse before starting. We got warmed up along the road in the controlled start.

This would be a great day ... riding my mare in her first 100, riding with friends and enjoying every mile on what promised to be a most perfect day weather-wise. My mare felt good, and I was glad to be in the saddle. Up Hickerson Hollow and down Land's Run we went. I was enjoying riding with Steph and Pete because all three of us had our doubts about our horses in May and now here we were, psyched and ready for the 100. We were all in great spirits.

I was a little suspicious about the river since there was hardly a mention about it at the pre-ride briefing. It was lovely ... and I was glad not to be on a shetland pony! Seeing Genie out there taking my picture is the highlight of my day (knowing full well that Genie is terrified of water!). I later heard that a few riders decided that a swim would feel good and went for it! We skimmed across and flew through Thunderbird Farms enjoying the ribbons that Dixie had helped me hang just a few days ago. Wait a minute ... I was going very fast on this first leg ... hummm ... I had told my intrepid and loyal pit crew (my sister and brother-in-law) to be at Fitchetts by 9am (as I had never gotten there before 9:30am. Up Veach and across the ridge to Milford. I had caught up with Adrienne, Anna, and Mathew along the ridge. Now I knew I was flying. Whee-ha. What a day.

So much for a pit crew ... I got to Fitchetts at 8:01! Holy moley. Now this is what it should be all about ... no less than 6-8 people offered me help ... food for me and my horse, water, etc. Lucky for me, Lynn Golemon was there (getting ready to ride drag from Fitchetts to Hickory) and once again saved my day! She, of course, had everything I needed on her trailer. Bill Golemon was there too and thanks to him, I had a horse holder who knew how to get my mare fed and rested. Lynn supplied me with electrolytes, and sports drink, feed, and hay for my mare. I was elated to be moving along so well at this point. Having ridden Tevis with Adrienne and Anna last year, I knew that we shared a liking for the same nutrition drink, so I was able to get a Boost from them! Everyone was so nice and helpful, and it was a fun stop. Back in the saddle and out just a minute behind the twins and Mathew, who kindly waited for me in the creek, cooling their horses' feet. Off, we rode. This was getting better and better.

Even the 6 miles of gravel road seemed pleasant because rain had left the road soft and it was a beautiful day, cool and no humidity. We turned left and headed up Habron hoping to catch the mountain laurel bushes in bloom at the top. Well, you can't have everything … only about 10% of the laurel was in bloom for us, but the pink and white flowers are gorgeous, especially since you have to climb so far to see them! The trail is very nice along the ridge. I had not seen this trail for 2 years and time has really improved it (time and a lot of rock pitching by Larry and others!). It was most pleasant … until Anna, riding one of Adrienne's horses, Pearly, asked me to check her shoes, as I was just behind her. Uh oh, Pearly was missing his right front shoe. Anna was off and had an Easy Boot (kind of a spare tire) in place in just a few minutes. Whew. He felt ok with the boot on and off we went. We boogied on into Roosevelt after what seemed a long time. We kept asking Mathew "How much farther?" He kept saying "soon"! We got there in good time actually and I was elated to see my faithful pit crew there and ready. I was very pleased that my mare passed this check in good shape. Hey, this is kind of fun having a horse that can move along! Sadly, Anna had some bad news here … Pearly had run a nail in his foot when he lost his shoe, and he was now out. I felt so bad for her since she had come from NM to try for a buckle, and it was such fun to be riding with Adrienne and Anna again. Adrienne and Mathew had left a minute ahead of me and I had to play catchup for a mile or so. We slowed down just a bit through the double dipper because of rocks, the horses wanting to drink a lot and horses starting to feel the miles. The ride over Scothorn was pleasant because Mathew gave us a running commentary on where the trail used to come and go. It is improved now, and it was quite nice. My mare was glad when the climbing was over, and we started down. We mostly cantered the

Chrisman Hollow Rd and were happy to turn back into the woods when we did. We all dismounted about ¼ mile before Hickory and our horses all recovered quickly.

My pit crew had to leave, so my friend, Dixie, was there for me. Thank goodness. It was here that my ride was over. My mare was a bit off in her right hind. Thank goodness for good vets as I had not felt, nor could I see a thing. Poor girl ... Mathew said it was most likely a pulled muscle, about the size of my small finger. See, a free diagnosis from lots of helpful vets!

Now, the truth ... I had really ridden about as far as I needed to that day. My mare and I kind of gave out about the same time. I was tired. It would have been fun to continue, but I had some pressing matters. Adrienne and Mathew went on to finish in the Top 10 (again) and I was tickled for them. I would like to thank Tom Sites for hauling my mare back to the 4H Center. Tom had already made 3 trips and it was just darn nice of him to take me. Actually, as it turned out, Tom was very glad to have made the trip back to the 4H Center because it was there that we learned of Mary Murphy's win in the 50-mile ride! Tom had sold Mary that horse and I think he went off to find her and demand more money! Hey folks, Tom has sold several OD winning horses to people!

I had a great day, proving once again that a finish is not always the best reward. I called this my Mom's Memorial Ride, and I loved the 55 miles as much as any I've ever done. It was my Mom who gave me my love of horses (I always say I came by it genetically as Mom's Dad raised horses and she had always loved them). We had last ridden together in AZ when Mom was 82 yrs old! I would be attending Mom's Memorial service the next day ... she died at age 96 on May 29 and this ride was for her! She taught me that you don't necessarily have to finish to win! Thanks Mom.

I would like to thank all the OD family and friends who lent me support this year. It is a good support system that gives one strength at times of loss. All the hugs, kind thoughts and the card were most appreciated.

2003
WESTERN ADVENTURE

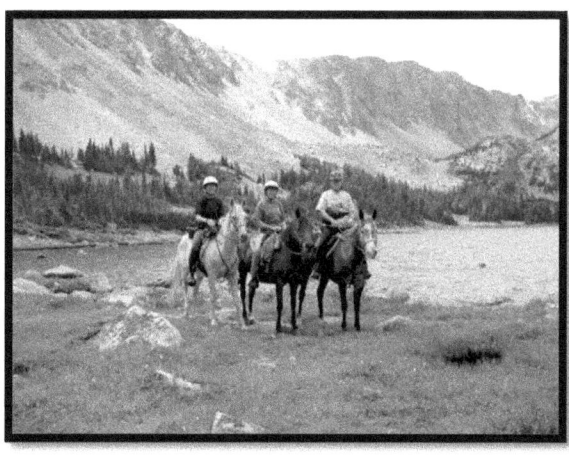

Paula on Randa, Rosie on Blu, and Lynn on Wonder in the Beartooth Mountains in Montana

A lot of people think I'm nuts, but I think a lot of them are just envious. Every summer I load up my horses, dog, and a cat or two and head west on an adventure. I think it all started with some cousins who retired to the high country of Colorado and built a gorgeous log home. When I went to see them, on a car trip with my Mother, I knew that I would someday have to spend time in the Rocky Mountains.

I eventually bought a secluded 40 acres with a small log cabin (for really cheap!) and more importantly, a beautiful, babbling creek where my horses could water. I had thought that I would hide out there every summer to escape the heat and humidity back east and write the great American novel. But, instead of the book, the property became my project! I had to fence off a few acres to keep the open range cattle away. I added a living room to the cabin, a septic field and an inside toilet (it's a girl thing). Then, I built a 12 x 24 ft. barn with a loft for my horses to stand under in the sleet and snow squalls. You have to love no electricity, no running water, no phone and only a woodstove for heat to appreciate this getaway spot.

All my animals loved the cool temperatures at 9000 feet. 30-degree nights and 60-degree days are perfect for us. My horses grew fat and fit on the rich, high-country grass. My dog and cats loved chasing chipmunks. I loved the simple life, the long nights, and the peace and quiet. As a hardworking trauma nurse the rest of the year, I felt that I deserved this escape. It was very healing and relaxing.

One year I decided to do something a bit different. Reading Trail Rider magazine had inspired me. I wanted to see some different places. As it turned out, I took a 10-week, 8000-mile trip with my 2 horses, 1 dog and 1 cat in my gooseneck trailer with only a dressing room. I loved camping and after 12 years of staying at my old cabin, this seemed a comfy and modern way to travel.

The adventure took shape when some friends from home (WV) told me they would be in Red Lodge, Montana, visiting relatives, on a certain date in August. They invited me to a party there! My neighbor and good friend, Lynn, cautiously asked me if I would ever let someone travel with me on my western jaunts? Hummm ... could be fun, but I had to think about it. I like being my own wagon boss. What the heck, OK; Lynn would take her own rig, also a gooseneck with a dressing room, 1 horse and 2 dogs.

We did not do much planning. I like spontaneity. Lynn packed the kitchen sink and we had all we needed! We left our homes in WV on different days, agreeing to meet up in Lexington, KY (where Lynn's daughter lived). And so, our adventure began on July 24. This is not the kind of adventure for you if you worry about where you will stop with 3 horses, 3 dogs and a kitty! I do not agonize, and I am very flexible. I love the expression "I love it when a plan comes together." It always does if you are easily satisfied and not a complainer. Being a happy, upbeat person out to have fun is my mantra.

We had a fun first stop in Lexington; KY. Lynn's daughter had made arrangements for a place to put our horses. We put up electric pens to keep our horses separate. It was quite hot, so we took the dogs and the cat to her daughter's animal-friendly home (fenced yard and A/C in the house). The movie Seabiscuit was premiering that day, so we went to see that. How perfect was that? A racehorse movie in Lexington, KY (although Seabiscuit never raced there)! The next day we took 2 of our horses to the Kentucky Horse Park and rode the beautiful grounds there. Lynn and I are endurance riders and no doubt we looked a bit odd to all the hunter/jumper and show pony folks. We rode past jumps that looked like they would keep elephants in! Yikes.

We left KY and headed to IL and the Shawnee National Forest. I had done an endurance ride there several years earlier and will never forget the awesome rock formations there. I had wanted to return and ride the trails for pleasure. We have a friend who conveniently lives right smack in the middle of the forest. We went to her place and camped there for 4 days. We rode in the Shawnee Forest 3 days from our friend's place and saw scenery that you will not see anyplace else in the USA. Caves that you can ride your horse right into. Trails that seem to disappear into rock walls, with just a narrow passage you can barely squeeze through. Cool creeks, waterfalls and rocks the size of office buildings. We saw a natural arch and a buffalo pictograph. Fantastic. The July weather was blistering but it was 10-15 degrees cooler in the deep wooded forest and very pleasant. And a cool shower in our friend's house, followed by a scrumptious supper made each day perfect! There are several ponds on my friend's property and my 1 yr old dog, Montana, (named for my upcoming destination as I had just acquired her 2 weeks before the trip) had lots of fun trying to catch the huge frogs who stayed 2 jumps ahead of her.

We said farewell to IL and drove our longest day (523 miles) up to eastern Nebraska. Now that we were west of the Mississippi river, we could count on finding horse-friendly fairgrounds for the night. Be aware however that I have found that some fairgrounds have converted from livestock to car racing and there are no pens left. We stayed at the Otoe Fairgrounds at Syracuse, NE and met some real nice 4H folks who welcomed us. There was no charge, and we were so happy about the stalls, water, and manure pit, that we made a donation to the 4H club. We always clean up after ourselves and leave a place cleaner than we found it. We want these places to always welcome us!

Lynn and I kept in touch while driving with a set of those little walkie-talkies so we could point out and share sights, gas stops, photo-ops, etc. "Can you hear me now?" We boogied across Nebraska, stopping at Gothensburg where I had to show Lynn the old pony express building. I just love to stop there with my horses. I park under the shade trees and drop the horse windows down so the horses can put their heads out. Tourists pet them and think it fitting that horses would be at a pony express stop! You can get your cards and letters postmarked with the old pony express stamp there and mailed to envious friends back home. Very historic stuff. After all, this was to be an educational as well as a pleasure trip!

That night we had the pleasure of staying at another friend's ranch, The North Eighty, in western Nebraska. We put up electric pens and our horses had lush grass and lots of wind to keep the bugs off. Lynn and I had showers and our dogs had lots of freedom. Our friend's home has 360-degree views and Lynn was busy taking pictures of sunsets and sunrises. Beautiful! We got to drive to a place just a few miles away and see part of the Oregon Trail that now passes through a private ranch.

With some helpful guidance from our friends (as well as a hot tip from a lady we chatted with at the Otoe Fairgrounds), we were directed to northwestern Nebraska, to the historic Fort Robinson. This had been a remount station in operation from 1874 until 1948 and is now a State park and National historic site. For many years there had been over 22,000 horses at this fort. The brick and log buildings are beautifully restored, and the horse barns and showgrounds are very nice. You can feel the history here! Lynn and I did not want to keep our horses in stalls and then have to camp a half mile from them, so we drove 6 miles north on a gravel road to the Nebraska National forest where we found big cattle pens, water, toilet facilities in a beautiful and secluded location between some pine hills. We had the whole place to ourselves. Our horses enjoyed the large pens, and we camped right beside them. We saddled up early the next morning and rode the historic "Trooper Trail" which was ridden by cavalry riders 100 years before. We rode past old officer quarters and club houses, across creeks and up to where we had gorgeous views of the surrounding hills. The area used to be all pine forested, but a devastating fire took most of the trees about 25 yrs ago, so we were riding across open grasslands. We saw buffalo and longhorn cattle! It was quite hot during the day, so we went down to the Fort in the afternoon to look around under the shade of huge cottonwood trees. We saw the officers quarters, the barns, the veterinary building and enjoyed a nice lunch in a little restaurant in one of the restored buildings.

We loved our seclusion and privacy at this nice spot, but we had a date to keep in Montana, so we headed west into Wyoming and into the Big Horn Mountains. We went to Buffalo, WY, picked up some forest service maps (and required weed free hay) and drove 13 miles west to the Hunter Trailhead in the Big Horns. This was a busy trailhead, but we got 3 pens for our horses and enjoyed watching the packers come and go. Outfitters take people out, drop them off with camping gear and then come back for them 4-5 days later. Folks enjoy the ride, then they camp, fish, swim in the lakes and relax. We set up our little camp tables, washstand, cookstove and fixed our supper. We enjoyed meeting and chatting with other campers and riders. We witnessed a sunset that at first looked like a forest fire! Drop dead stunning! Lynn got a picture.

The next morning, we saddled up and headed off to Seven Brothers Lakes, riding higher and higher into the mountains on very rocky trails. Our horses were shod. Sure enough, we counted 7 lakes on our way up, each one more pristine than the last. We missed seeing a moose by minutes at a small pond some other riders told us. Darn. That was one beautiful ride ... from the knees up ... a bit too rocky for me. Next time I would go to the trails over by Shell, WY, on the western side of the Big Horn mountains.

The next day we broke camp (it takes us about 10 minutes to load up and get underway) and drove north into Montana, big sky country. We made a stop at the Custer battlefield historic site, but only walked about for about 30 minutes as we were not allowed to let our animals out of the trucks, and it was hot. We found a campground called 7th Ranch which borders the National park land. Here we met Chip, the campground/ranch owner who led us on a wonderful trailride across his ranch while pointing out the logistics of the Custer battle. It was a private tour and since Chip used to teach history in the local schools and grew up here, he knew his history. It was Chip's birthday, and he was treating himself to a birthday ride on his very nice Morab gelding. These are beautiful, rolling grasslands and we had a nice breeze.

We left the 7th Ranch just in time to hit Billings, MT right at the time a girlfriend was flying in to meet us. It was 105 degrees at the airport, so we just pulled up to the terminal and our friend came out the door and got in Lynn's truck. Since I travel with 2 horses, we have friends who joined us along the way, to share in our adventure for 5-7 days each. Paula was the first to join us. We got out of blistering Billings and went 60 miles south to Red Lodge where it was a little cooler. As I mentioned before, we are flexible about our animals and in Red Lodge we contacted a friend of a friend and he found us a place where our horses could be in stalls at a huge indoor arena where it was cool. We took a motel room to enjoy showers, running water, swimming pool, hot tub, A/C, and breakfasts! Split 3 ways it's easily affordable! It was here that we met our friends from back east and we partied the next several days with their wonderful family. We met some real nice Red Lodge folks. We did a nice day trip by car one day over Beartooth Pass. If you have never done that, put it on the list of top 10 places to see in the USA. Lynn and Paula had never seen this before and they were blown away with the scenery. We got out and walked in snow at 10,000 ft and Lynn took pictures of the wildflowers that hang on somehow in the wind. We were loving the cold temps! We nearly froze on top of that pass, and it was a delight. We camped and rode our horses 4 days in the Beartooths and slept under blankets every night. How many beautiful creeks and waterfalls can one take in? High mountain lakes, beautiful trails, and moose! Yikes. Even a hailstorm to get our attention.

Now sometimes plans don't work out and you must go to plan B. We had hoped to go camp and ride in the Pryor Mtns and look for Cloud, the wild, palomino stallion, but 103-degree temps foiled that plan. It was just too hot to camp and there was no shade in the area, so we had to scrap that plan. Alas, after a week of fun with friends, riding, camping, dining, shopping, and sightseeing, we had to put Paula back on a plane and Lynn and I made our way south back into Wyoming.

We stumbled on a nice camping spot in the Chief Joseph area just north of Cody. It was on some private ground, but a nice guy (a Federal employee) told us we could stay there. There were some nice big Forest Service cattle pens and grass, high atop a plateau. Much cooler than down in the lowland campground. We learned that we were in wolf and grizzly country and met 2 Federal workers who were studying recent wolf kills. They even supplied us with water and told us a good place to ride. Of course, they also warned us about bears! Yikes. Two of our dogs accompanied us on most of our rides, so we felt pretty safe. Ha, ha. When we set out on our horses, we were a bit apprehensive about bears, but by the time we returned 4 hours later, we were feeling pretty brave, having not seen a bear!

One night we witnessed a top ten full moonrise over Heart Peak. Wow! I wrote a zillion friends post cards to tell them about that spot and then, I mailed them as we drove through Cody the next day. We drove south through the Wind River Canyon and then west to Dubois, WY. We stayed with some really nice friends there and enjoyed nice showers in a real bathroom. Washing up out of a pan is ok, but a nice hot shower once a week is heavenly. Our friends took us on an all-day trail ride in the Pinnacle Peaks area, north of the Tetons. Oh, such scenery! We were dwarfed by the massive cliff faces and peaks. We rode past gorgeous, high mountain lakes with names like Upper and Lower Jade, and they were a most beautiful shade of emerald, green. We picnicked high above one beautiful lake. Lynn and I took a day here to drive into Jackson, WY where we went to see the new movie Open Range. We could relate to that story as we were sort of "free grazing" our way across the west! We stopped to watch the beavers at work and photographed the sunset over the Tetons. We also saw buffalo, elk and mule deer that day. Dubois was a fun stop.

Time constraints and forest fires prevented us from taking our horses any further west, like into Yellowstone or the Tetons. Another time. We had to head back east and camped a few days in the Medicine Bow Mountains in southeast WY. We stopped at the National Forest headquarters to get maps, so we would have some idea where to camp and trails to ride. We unfortunately camped illegally at one place because the sign directing horse campers was down (knocked down by range cattle)! Since we were the only folks there, the Forest employee said it was ok, but we moved to a better place at Pelton Creek.

There were horse pens and fire rings there and nice, shady camping spots. We had this place all to ourselves too. We rode through some gorgeous pine and aspen forests and crossed the North Platte River where our dogs had to swim! We rode along Douglas Creek and found endless trails. I had been on a 5-day endurance ride in this same area about 8 years earlier and remembered the nice trails. They are snow mobile routes in the winter.

We dropped south and into Colorado over Willow Creek Pass, south of Waldon. We went into Grand county, CO, one of the most scenic areas of Colorado and stayed at my cousin's. We rode our horses out to the area where my little cabin was located and visited some friends who also have a cabin nearby. We rode up, pulled our saddles, turned our horses into the lush meadow and partied on the deck with my friends. We never made it to my old cabin because an afternoon storm was brewing. We saddled up and rode back (at an endurance pace) to where we had left the trailer. As soon as we got the horses loaded, the heavens opened, and it poured for the next 12 hours. The next day, after the rain, we went to soak in the hot springs at Hot Sulphur Springs. That felt wonderful! Wild horses and Native Americans had used these springs for centuries before they were bought and operated commercially.

We now had another date to keep. Our second girlfriend, Odette, was to join us for 5 days at a friend's ranch near Larkspur, CO. This is a 400-acre horse ranch that backs up to the Pike National Forest. Lynn and I remained there for 8 days and enjoyed 5 days with our friend from California. We had some nice rides in that red rock country and enjoyed hot tub soaks, dinners on the deck and a massage or two. Wicked. The ranch owner, an endurance rider, sells arabian endurance horses. We got to ride lots of different horses during our stay. There were about 90 horses there, some for sale and some boarders. We even ran into an endurance friend from back east. Old home week.

We remained at this busy and awesome ranch through the Labor Day weekend, as we did not want to try going to horse camps or get into heavy traffic over that holiday. We then moved about 30 miles north to the Indian Creek Equestrian Campground in the Pike National Forest. We enjoyed a nice couple of days there, having the whole place to ourselves again. Timing is everything. We rode some very beautiful forest trails and even got up onto the Colorado Trail and rode a few miles of that (pretty rocky footing). That trail runs from Denver to Durango, all above 10,000 feet!

It was here that Lynn and I had to part company after a glorious and fun 5 weeks of travel. She had to return home for some previous commitments, and I had to head up to my cabin to watch the aspen turn gold. We celebrated our last night with a nice campfire and a beans & franks supper. Do we know how to party or what?!

The next morning, we said goodbye and thought it remarkable that we were still the best of friends after all these adventures. Lynn headed east and I headed back to Grand county. My horses were glad to get up to the cabin to enjoy some freedom, good grass, a nice creek, and their barn. The cat felt right at home, as he had been going to that cabin for 13 years. My dog enjoyed chasing chipmunks. I settled in and caught up with my friends and neighbors to get caught up on all the news. I got some rest after my first 5 weeks on the road.

My third girlfriend, Dixie, was to join me here for a week. She drove out from Virginia with her 2 dogs and she had even more travel plans as well. She arrived on Sept. 14, and we had a fun week of riding, hiking, cutting firewood, finding a farrier and visiting my cousins. We stayed active and enjoyed the 20-degree nights and 60-degree days. We loaded up horses, dogs and the cat and went up to the Medicine Bows in WY, where Lynn and I had camped in August. I wanted Dixie to see that pretty area and I wanted to ride more of the nice trails. An extra bonus was that now the aspen were starting to turn gold. We had a nice day ride there through pine and aspen forests. It sure makes one appreciate our National Forests! Again, we had this camp to ourselves ... except for the magnificent bull moose that walked right through our camp! Yikes.

Dixie then headed on north to meet up with a friend in Montana. They went to look for Cloud, the wild mustang stallion, in the Pryor mountains and they saw him! They had a much cooler time than I'd had up there in August.

I remained at my little cabin and watched the aspen reach full gold glory. A beautiful time in the Colorado Rockies. Then, I packed up and headed away on Sept. 27 and headed for South Dakota which would be my 7th state to ride in. Dixie and I had made arrangements to meet at a campground that we had read about in Trail Rider magazine. We both pulled into Plenty Star Ranch about the same time, got the horses settled (and blanketed) in nice pens, and went out for a good supper where Dixie told me all about searching for and finding Cloud in MT. I was a bit envious! We were surprised when the temp dropped to 20 that night. I have a propane heater in my trailer and Dixie, who was camping in her truck, had to start the engine, and run the heater to get warm in the morning. The campground has a nice, warm, and clean bath house.

Plenty Star Ranch raises some unique mustangs, cute and tough looking. Dixie and I saddled up and had a nice 4-hour ride right from the ranch.

I wanted Dixie to see historic Fort Robinson too and since it was on our way south, we made plans to go there. On our way we stopped at Hot Springs, SD to tour the Mamouth Site. Very interesting dig! They have uncovered lots of mamouths and other prehistoric animals. Now that the weather was cooler, we could stop and leave animals on the trailer and in our trucks. We drove south through Wind Cave Park where we stopped to watch prairie dogs going about their business. We also saw buffalo along that stretch. We got to Ft. Robinson and headed out to the same nice spot where Lynn and I had camped. Nice pens and places to camp. We had the place to ourselves probably because of the 20-degree night temps! It was good sleeping weather. The next day we rode the Boots and Saddle trail and were sure that some of the rocks we saw were mamouth teeth! We had just learned about them in Hot Springs. It was windy and chilly out on the hills, but it was nice to see the foliage in fall color now.

After a cold ride, we decided to load up and keep heading south and east. We made it to Ogallala, Nebraska that night and camped at the nice fairgrounds. We put the horses in a large pen and crawled into our beds just as it began raining. I slept well but awoke at first light to find my horses shivering. I put blankets on them and put them in the trailer and they warmed up quickly, eating their breakfast. The rain changed to snow! Dixie and I drove to MacDonalds for breakfast and felt giddy about the first snow.

The snow soon changed back to rain as we headed east on I-80. In fact, we were soon in lovely, warm sunshine. We were to get together with some friends near Omaha that evening. I found a horse motel near Papillion and left the horses there while we went to our friend's place where we enjoyed a nice hot meal and showers. Our friends are in the military and were stationed there.

Dixie and I parted company again as she wanted to do some sightseeing and I wanted to get into Illinois to visit my cousins. My Mother was from Bond Co. Illinois, and I have a lot of cousins there.

They have nice farms and can usually find a place for my horses. It takes me a few days to get around and visit them all, but I enjoy seeing them each year. I know they think I'm nuts!

Dixie and I met up again (as we were both heading east) and traveled to Indiana where we camped and rode in the beautiful Clark State Forest. It was begun as an experimental forest in 1904 and you can see a lot of different and unusual trees there. We stayed at the equestrian camp and rode some very nice trails. Endurance rides are held here but we mostly encountered pleasure riders on spiffy horses. We were getting pretty far east, and I was dismayed to see a lot of riders chatting on their cell phones as they rode! You won't see that out west as there are no cell towers in the National Forests! I prefer the remote to the civilized!

Dixie then headed for home in VA, but I made one more stop in Greenbrier Co, WV to ride some of the Greenbrier Trail, a rail-to-trail path beside the Greenbrier River. A very scenic trail. When I ride alone, I take both horses and switch tack every now and then so both horses get ridden. The spare horse just follows along. My dog loves to go on trail rides. We rode about 20 miles where I enjoyed the colorful fall foliage before loading up for the last 4-hour haul to home.

A 10-week odyssey that I will treasure forever. I rode my horses in 9 states, over a dozen National Forests and 1 State Park. I rode 34 of the 75 days. I went 8000 miles and spent $1020.00 on gas. I loved every mile! I could not wait to get home and put all my photos in an album so that I could share some of the beauty and joy with friends. If you have a horse and trailer, I urge you to take to the road, if you love trail riding. There are a lot of great trails out there to be enjoyed and preserved.

SANDHILLS RIDE BY HORSEBACK (2009)

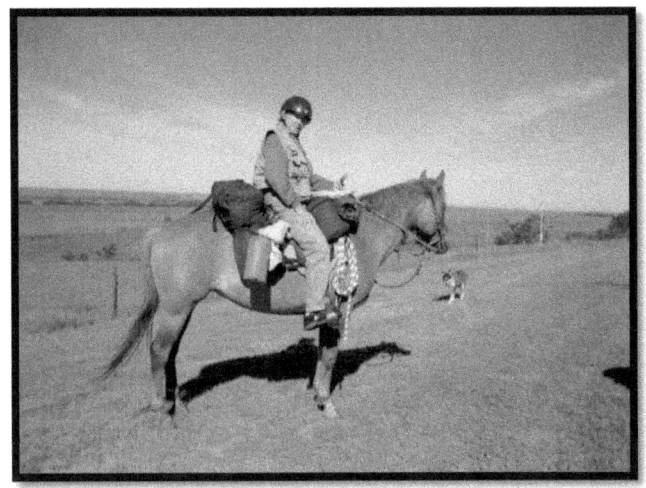

Rosie on Maple in Nebraska

The welcome sign read: "May peace be with you while you stay, And joy be with you on your way." That is exactly what I found when I rode my horse through northwestern Nebraska ... wonderful, warm, and welcoming folks who allowed me to stay and nothing but beauty along my way through the sand hills and pine ridge forests.

I had originally wanted to ride my horse from the Atlantic to the Pacific, as many "long riders" have done. A long rider being defined as someone who rides a horse at least 1000 miles (without having a truck/trailer/camper along for support). Being from the east, I had doubts about even attempting to ride from the Atlantic even to the Mississippi River with so many paved and busy roads. Now, west of the Mississippi looked a lot more promising as there are wonderful gravel/dirt back roads in the west. I even had a friend in NE who had a 34-mile driveway!! Now that is my kind of country. Ranches of thousands of acres were something I could only dream about.

To turn a dream into a reality takes motivation and determination. I had done a short 8-day test ride with my horse, camping each night as I covered 100 miles in a National Forest not far from my home. That went well and other than being out there during the first week of bear season (yikes), it all was great fun. I do love to trail ride.

I packed up my rig and drove to western NE, to Lewellen, near Ash Hollow Park, where I would leave it while I did my short, long ride. I had given a lot of thought as to what I would need to carry: tent, food for dog, horse and me, stove, clothes, rain gear, towel/soap ... and that was about it. It helps to be a minimalist in this endeavor. I had gone over some possible plans for a ride route, wanting at first to ride a circular route that would take me south, then west to Chimney Rock, then north to Fort Robinson, then back southeast through the sand hills. My hosts, Butch being a native Nebraskan, suggested that I just ride northwest from their place, through the sand hills to Fort Robinson. That turned out to be just what I did, and it was the perfect route for my first short, long ride.

There was a great deal of laughter as I actually packed up my horse that first day, June 16. My mare, Maple, is very tolerant which I think is a wonderful trait in a long riders' mount. She does not care what I put on top of her! Not just any horse can do this. I loaded saddle pad, saddle, front saddle bags, rear saddle bags, a cantle bag behind the saddle and a tent on the front of the saddle. Part of the challenge for me was that I do not ride in a full western saddle with wide skirts and places to tie to; I ride a "Sports Saddle" which only weighs 11 lbs. I used this saddle successfully for the past 15 yrs in the sport of endurance. Oh yes, that is what I used to do ... race my horse 50-100 miles in a day. Maple and I were well suited for sane, slow trail days now. Roughly, I figured that Maple was carrying about 220 lbs when I was in the saddle (the saddle, pad and I weigh 168 lbs). I rode out at 8:30am on a beautiful 60-degree day, heading northwest through the sand hills of NE, accompanied by my faithful dog, Tana.

We rode 13 miles that first day and camped that night at the elander Ranch. Let me just say that the best part of my ride was meeting such nice folks all along the way. This ranch has been in this family for 6 generations which is a pretty impressive statistic! Their huge stone barn with walls 3 feet thick was over 100 yrs old. These busy ranchers welcomed me and even got into the act on day 2 by helping me solve some of the pack load distribution and tie down problems. Again, lots of laughter as I packed up and rode out with several new ties holding my packs in place (they tended to shift).

Day 2: We went through the Peterson Ranch, another beautiful and huge ranch, where I met Dan, the foreman, who greeted me and even opened gates for me! He told me that Maple would carry me well on this ride because she was a red dun (Dan happened to own 3 red duns I think)! Kay, the owner, even stopped to say hi as I rode through the ranch. Everyone was so nice!

We did 19 miles on day 2, which took its toll on all 3 of us in the heat. Note: there are no shade trees in the sand hills! We watered at cow tanks but kept moving in hopes of finding a creek with some shade. Ah ha ... we came to a beautiful creek on a ranch owned by the Morman church. I learned that they have bought up a number of ranches in the area and have thousands of cattle.

This one was originally part of the huge Eldred Ranch. We welcomed the cool creek water and the shade of the huge cotton woods. A perfect spot to camp. We rested. Soon, stock trailers began to pull in near me and lots of horses were being readied. I learned that there was to be branding the next day! I was welcomed to watch, help, and eat with the cowboys. The ranch manager came out to welcome me and said that I was more than welcome to camp. He said, "Little Lady, we don't get many visitors out here, so the ones we get, we like to treat them right!" I was treated "right" for sure. He offered his house phone/internet/shower and

I assured him that I was doing this ride to get away from phones and internet, but I would take him up on a shower. I decided to stay over a day here to let my dog rest.

Day 3 was the brandin' ... a most efficient operation. 50 cowboys/wranglers/buckaroos roped/dragged/branded 1000 calves in 5 hours.

This was followed by a wonderful luncheon put on by the gals at the managers home. A good time was had by all. Maple loved having so many horse buddies nearby and Tana spent the day resting. It was a great place to camp.

Day 4 took us into the Crescent Lake Wildlife Refuge area where ducks and grouse kept Maple on her toes as we rode along. No shade but lots of good, lush grass for Maple. I kept busy opening gates at all the cattle guards in the ranching country. At a lot of the guards there are 3 gates to open and close to leave the road and return to it. Partway through the refuge area, I came to the Dietlein Ranch, where a very nice lady, Nancy, allowed me to camp despite the fact that she was leaving to be away a few days! This lady knew my hosts, so I had good references! Because this was summer, the cattle pens were empty, so I had a place to put Maple at night throughout my ride. I would hand graze Maple on a lead and then put her in a big pen at night where she had good water.

Day 5 took us onto another Morman ranch where there were lots of cattle and biting bugs. We came bucking and kicking to the old Eldred Ranch. No one was around and I put maple in a stall in a cattle barn to get her into shade and out of the bugs. I just waited for someone to arrive before I set up camp. I never presumed that I could stay unless someone told me that it was OK. Over the afternoon, several folks came in ... the mail lady, Bev, then, Cordell and Cierra, & Reed who all work for the Morman Ranches. They all assured me that I could stay there, no problem. I even took refuge in the big house during a thunderstorm!

Day 6, a Sunday, found us on the old oil road, 155, heading north. Uh oh, we had a flat tire! Lost a shoe! Maple cannot travel without a shoe, and I carry 2 spares, rubber overshoes called Easy Boots. I slipped one on the barefoot and we rode on. I made it about 18 miles that day to the Beck Ranch where I was fortunate to meet Cindy & John because they had a farrier coming the next day! That was an extreme stroke of good luck for me. These folks were so nice that I did not even have to pitch my little tent, for they had a small camper trailer to stay in. That was really nice as we had a couple of severe thunderstorms the 2 nights I was there. Sure enough, on Monday, the farrier came and gave Maple a new set of shoes. Yea, we were back in business.

Let me interject here that I have proven that without a refrig or pantry to go to, one can and will lose weight! I was doing well on my oatmeal & tea breakfast, my jerky and raisin lunches and chicken soup or pasta noodles for supper. Few desserts! Maple, Tana, and I were feeling fit and healthy. However, as my trip progressed, and all the nice folks took me in, I began to eat a lot more! They all fed me! I think I started gaining weight!

While I was at the Beck Ranch, 3 friends (Louie, Ernie, and Sherri) from Lewellen drove up to find me, bringing coolers of food (fruit, brownies, sandwiches, and drinks) and we had a fun reunion. As it turned out, a lot of these NE folks know each other, so everyone made me feel very at home. I was still in Garden County (the largest of NE counties) after a week of riding! My friends were caught in a bad thunderstorm going back home that night and the tables were turned ... I was worried about them on washed out roads!

While at the Beck Ranch I asked Cindy if she had something to read while I waited a day for the farrier. She gave me a very interesting book, Vanishing Dreams, about the history of Lisco, NE written by her Uncle, Wm. Vogel!

That was a fun read and had lots of really historic pictures of local places. I was tickled to get to read that one!

Day 8: After a wonderful breakfast and send off from the Beck Ranch, I rode north and out of Garden County. Yesterday was the summer solstice and the longest daylight of the year! I felt great! I rode to a ranch up along rt. 20 near Antioch. I had met Janice and Brady yesterday when they had come to fetch some cows of theirs at the Beck Ranch and they had invited me to stop at their place the next night. Janice had me stay in her home and fed me well! Brady went over maps with me to direct me on old trails heading west towards Alliance, so that I would not have to ride along busy Rt. 20, beside the railroad tracks! While spending almost a day with Janice, I got to ride with her (in a truck) to take 2 bulls to Rushville! Wow, we stopped at several stores and everything! Civilization!

Day 9: I rode out back through their ranch and along Rt. 20 for about 2 miles, then turned north on a gravel road from which I picked up the old trail that Brady had told me about. That was really neat ... through cow pastures with water tanks and a few wire gates. No roads or sounds of civilization at all ... nice. I was now riding west. I came out on a ranch that had some horses! Maple said "yea!" We found a shade tree and stopped for lunch. I found my way out of that field and into a ranch where Jim told me I was welcome to camp. Again, I was able to put Maple in a cool, shady, big old barn where she could enjoy some coolness and shade. I pitched my little tent in a nice, mowed area by a gate and cooked my supper. Just as it was ready, about 50 heifers and a bull came up to see what I was doing!! I had to move my tent and dinner to the other side of a gate!

Day 10: I rode out at 7am and got on the paved road to Alliance. Jim had directed me to look for the Alliance Veterinary Clinic that I would see just as I arrived in town. That was very helpful as I was able to leave Maple in a pen there while did some shopping. Tana got to enjoy the AC in the vet clinic! Lucky dog! I enjoyed Safeway, a Mexican restaurant,

Dairy Queen, and cell service! We had come 95 miles, and this was the first town we had come to. I restocked my oatmeal and soup. This turned out to be another lucky day for me; it was the day of the annual Festival of the Fountain. I walked to join hundreds of other folks in the celebration. The fountain is glorious! It shoots 70 feet high in several different patterns (and colors after dark)! It is beautiful. I also toured the Knight's Museum, dedicated to the military. There was a brass band, a cowboy poet & his wife, and a rock band. Hotdogs, ice cream and sodas too. I walked back to my animal companions and spent the night out behind the vet clinic. They were very nice to allow us to stay and even gave Maple some wonderful hay. When I tried to pay for that, the vet said to just do some good deed for someone else and pay it forward! I did that. Alliance was a fun stop.

Day 11: I rode north out of town at 5:30am to avoid morning traffic along the paved road. I rode to Ross' farrier shop (he was the man who had put shoes on Maple a few days before). He directed me across some fields to where I could pick up the county gravel, back roads that would take me north and west. We had a wonderful ride to Borea on the back roads, heading north and west. I rode into Pat & Bob's place which was a wonderful stop. Married 62 years, these folks are special. I had to leave there after they fed me delicious meals before I grew too fat and lazy! Maple, Tana, and I were getting used to trains by now, as we were sort of following the RR north. We had a little set back here when Tana "shaded up" under Bob's truck and got run over. She got a cut on a front leg which

I doctored and wrapped. As she was sore and a bit lame, I asked Bob to haul us north to Hemmingford where I could hole up at the Box Butte County Fairgrounds for a few days, letting Tana's cut heal and I could write several post cards and thank you notes. Bob took us right to the Fairgrounds and contacted the director to let her know that I would be there. Phyllis turned out to be another great contact and help as I camped at the Fairgrounds for 3 days (Days 12, 13, 14). She gave me directions for going on northwest.

Day 15: Tana was good to go, and we rode out of historic Hemingford (famous since 1800's for alfalfa seed and potatoes) at 6 am after a few days of food and rest. The road to Box Butte Reservoir is paved and I had to keep Tana on a leash for that stretch. Again, it was my lucky day when I met Jeannine and Tom at their ranch just south of the reservoir. There were a lot of storms at night, and I was fortunate to get to stay in the ranch house this night and got to meet some of their family. Such nice folks! I was loving Nebraska! Another wonderful feed and accommodation.

Day 16: Jeannine held Maple while I loaded up and I think was a bit amazed at how all the gear fit on top! We rode out at 6:45am. I was now riding along on a gravel road when a man drove toward me and stopped. He asked, "Is your butt sore?" I said no and we stood and chatted for 10 minutes. When he found out that I was riding to Fort Robinson, he told me to look up his daughter who works there as a wrangler! I would do that. We went about 12 miles, heading west, when I spotted a man mowing hay ... and he spotted me as well. As it turned out, I rode into his ranch to see if I could camp there. I just kind of hung out by the barns (I put Maple in an empty pen) and waited. I greeted several people who stopped in ... a cattle buyer, a neighbor wanting to use his phone and a weed man. I was the official greeter that day! Dave drove in on the hay mower about 3:30pm and said that I was welcome to camp overnight. Whew. He went out to bale hay and did so until 10:30pm! Long days. I pitched my tent under a carport/garage that night in case of storms.

Day 17: This day began early and with a scrumptious breakfast! Dave had fixed some sausage and eggs and invited me in to eat. That turned out to be a real treat for during breakfast Dave told me about his Grandfather, a Basque sheep herder who came to America back in 1912, as a young man. A wonderful book, titled Beltran, was written about him, published in 1979. I bought a copy of it when I got home and found it to be a wonderful read about a very interesting life lived in the American west. This was a lucky stop for me as a lover of books and true stories about the settling of our great country. I rode out at 7:30 am after an entertaining stop and good rest for Maple and Tana. Dave directed me to my next stop on the back roads, but I missed a turn and went about 8 extra miles that day. That was not good because it was a very hot day, and we did not need extra miles. Totally my fault but I got to enjoy more nice scenery, old schools, and a cemetery along the way. I stopped off at an abandoned farm where I found water and a shady barn for a couple of hours. What should have been a 2–3-hour ride turned out to be about a

10-hour day! We rode past the Butler Farrier School and on to our next stop at 6pm. A long and hot day. I was welcomed by Gloria who had been alerted by Dave that I was heading her way. She was delighted to have us stop and her dog and horses seemed excited to see us ride in. Gloria has a quaint little house tucked under shade trees and a big red barn and paddocks. This was a welcome sight. We were now on the edge of the pine ridge forest. Yea ... shade at last. Gloria was so darn nice that she persuaded me to stay 2 nights! We had a wonderful time visiting and had a lot to talk about. Gloria was from Baltimore, MD, not far from where I grew up and we are both registered nurses and knew the hospitals where we each had worked back east. Small world. I got a kick out of Gloria as she told me that her children tell her that she lives in the wilderness! My kind of living! I guess they all like city life. Not me. I was able to help Gloria a bit with moving heavy feed bags (horse, dog, and kitty) and some house maintenance. Our dogs had a good time although her young retriever had way too much energy for tired Tana that first day! It was a good rest stop for all of us. Again, I ate well while at Gloria's. We were a grateful trio. Once again, it was a lucky stop because Gloria insisted that I stay in the house, and we had terrible thunderstorms both nights.

Day 19: This was July 4th! I was glad to be far away from any town because Maple and Tana do not care for the noisy sounds of fireworks. I got off to a rather late start but since I was only riding 1 mile to my next stop, it did not seem like I needed to head out early! This was my shortest ride. Gloria had planned to go see a daughter in CO, so I moved on to a wonderful B&B just a mile down the road. The Schoolhouse B&B is a wonderful place for any traveler! I rode in there on July 4th and there were guests at the B&B, so I camped in the big red barn. Now this was something: this barn is a work of art to me. It was built by German brothers about 1916 and it is 115 feet long and 50 feet wide!! It has huge double tie stalls in it for 24 draft horses. It is yummy and a real treasure. Carol and Tom are the perfect innkeepeers as they are just really nice, warm folks who make one feel at home from the first moment.

They had gone into Crawford for the July 4th festivities, and I was asleep when they got home that night, so I did not meet them until the next morning. They knew that I was there though. I was soundly asleep in my tent pitched in the big barn. Carol was shocked that I camped in the barn, but I loved it!

Day 20: Carol walked down and invited me to come into breakfast with their B&B guests! How very nice! We got acquainted and had a very pleasant breakfast and visit. The B&B guests left that morning and Carol insisted that I stay the next night in the schoolhouse B&B house. It really is an old schoolhouse and the original blackboards on the walls are full of thank yous and greetings from the guests who have stayed there. Carol and Tom reside in the big farmhouse just next to the schoolhouse. They are not your average innkeepers because they love meeting folks who come and welcome them in for suppers too! Their whole place is really fun with lots of wild turkeys and their own domestic chickens and guineas, kitties, dogs, bunnies, and horses. It is a beautiful setting as well at the edge of the pine ridge. So, I stayed 2 nights at this quiet, safe, and delightful spot. Tom took me on a drive around the local area to show me the sights. He is a great tour guide and knows the local history! He showed me the Belmont School (now closed) where he and Carol had both taught. We drove through the old railroad tunnel, built 1920 and now a rail trail/road. This is a beautiful area, rolling hills, pine trees, and creeks. I was once again lucky in my timing for I got to attend the Wohler Ranch 125th celebration picnic! The Wohler Ranch is just a mile up the road from the B&B. We went there on Sunday afternoon and enjoyed a very pleasant and convivial picnic with about 100 people and enough food for an army! I got introduced to lots of nice folks who welcomed me. The weather was perfect, and the day was great fun. That evening Carol drove me over to meet Jaynet, down the road a few miles, where I would stay tomorrow night! Jaynet has a very interesting hideaway a mile off the county road and back through a wildlife refuge area. We crossed a creek 7 times on our drive into her place. What a secluded, shady, and special place. I would look forward to riding to her place tomorrow.

Day 21: After another wonderful breakfast at this B&B, I said goodbye to Tom who was heading out to spray weeds and Carol who was heading off to a 4H class, I got packed up and rode out at 10am. It was only about a 5-mile ride to Jaynet's. Maple, Tana, and I enjoyed that shady stretch of road with nice creeks alongside of it. A pleasant change from all the hot, treeless roads we had been on through the sand hills. We got to Jaynet's about 11:15 am after an easy ride. I picked up Jaynet's mail and carried that in her 1-mile lane, across the creeks, enjoying the huge shade trees. Jaynet welcomed me and since she has horses, she had a good accommodation for Maple. Jaynet's beautiful log home is set beside a lovely pond complete with ducks and lillies. Bunnies hop about and her horses look so picturesque grazing beside the pond. I loved her log home, which is custom, yummy and comfortable. Jaynet too had done nursing and was now a writer so once again, we had lots to talk about. I got to read some of her stories which were very entertaining. She put me up in a perfect little apartment just off her garage. It was perfect: living room, with an all-one- piece kitchen unit (sink, stove, refrig), bathroom and bedroom. I was getting spoiled about staying in my tent! Jaynet has a yard full of gorgeous flowers. She battles constantly to keep the wildlife from eating them all! People were spoiling us for sure. Gloria had dropped off goodies for Tana and me while I was at Carol's and then Carol left a rawhide treat for Tana while we were at Jaynet's.

Day 22: Jaynet twisted my arm and insisted that I stay another day/night so we could go out to dinner at the Cook Shack. OK, I would stick around although it was taking me a long time to make these last few miles into Crawford! It was another fun day. Carol, Jaynet and I went to Toadstool Park which was fascinating. Sandstone formations in very interesting and odd shapes. We hiked around and took lots of pictures. Then, we went to the Cook Shack where I enjoyed seeing the lovingly restored old town buildings that had been moved there and carefully rebuilt. It is like an old-time town with a store, a school, a jail, sheriff's office, livery, farrier shop, saloon, house, and barn. All 1800 buildings. I could have easily enjoyed living during that time! We stopped in Crawford, and they showed me how to ride through town to the rodeo grounds when I got there. That was very helpful. We had a fun day, and I was further spoiled and treated. Much appreciated.

Day 23: I got packed up, thanked Jaynet profusely and rode out at 6:30am heading to Crawford. The ladies had told me places where I might stop if I needed to, but we rode right on into Crawford. I had not camped in a town since Hemmingford and I needed to stop, write letters, and mail them. I stopped to visit with the saddle maker in town and then rode on to the rodeo grounds. They were deserted but still a bit muddy from all the rains that had hit on July 4th. I put Maple in a pen and stowed my gear. I walked back to town and went to the grocery and post office. I wrote and mailed a lot of cards from here. I walked back to the rodeo grounds, grazed Maple, wrote more cards, pitched my tent, and tried to stay cool. Jaynet and Carol drove in to find me! We had another nice visit. I couldn't thank them enough for all their kindness.

Day 24: I got up and enjoyed my oatmeal and tea. I fed Maple and Tana and let Maple graze while I cleaned up her pen and stowed my gear. I walked back to town and mailed more cards and ate more breakfast at the Frontier Restaurant before returning to the rodeo grounds. I loaded up and rode out at 9:30am heading to Fort Robinson. It would have been nice (not to mention safer) if I had been able to ride cross country along the Pine ridge Trail on to Fort Robinson State Park property, but the gates are locked, so I had to ride along Rt. 20 for 3 miles … whew. A busy highway. I reached the Fort at 10:30am and rode back toward the horse barn area. I had been here before, so I knew where I was to go. I had to unload all my gear and tack, put Maple in a stall and then go to the Park office to check in and get camping and stall permits. I met some very nice folks at the camp area and asked them if I could leave my gear with them while I checked in. Edna and Curt were camping there in their huge motor home, and they were delighted to help out. The Park people were not quite sure where I should put my "parking sticker/permit" since I came in by horse! I just posted it on my little tent. Tana was done. I took a great picture of her flat out in the grass, resting. Maple was fit and ready to go further. I was fit and fat from all the great meals I had been fed! We all 3 felt great after our 175 mile/24-day trip. I have nothing but fond memories of northwestern Nebraska from my short-long ride!

CENTENNIAL TRAIL RIDE : SOUTH DAKOTA

Diane on Rosie, the mule, and Rosie on Maple
at Bear Butte, South Dakota

After I had had a wonderful short-long ride (24 days) across the sand hills of Nebraska, riding my red dun mare, Maple, accompanied by my faithful dog, Tana, I decided that I loved this horse camping/riding and meeting the wonderful people of the plains. So, I searched for another destination and found the Centennial Trail through the Black Hills of South Dakota. I had never ridden any of it , nor had I talked to anyone who had, so this was a totally new adventure for me. In preparation, I called a friend whom I knew was somewhere in the Midwest with her mule. Diane is originally from Iowa and heads there every summer to see her relatives. We both live in West Virginia where we ride together. I called Diane on her cell phone and asked her if she would like to ride and camp the Centennial Trail with me. She would! Since my dog, Tana, was still resting up from our ride across the sand hills a month earlier, I substituted Diane and her mule for Tana! Tana would rest at a friend's ranch in Nebraska while I tackled another 100 miles of trail in South Dakota. I think that was fine with Tana as she got to enjoy a lovely, air-conditioned home and two Corgi friends (Junie and Andy) while I was away.

Diane and I met up at the Broken Arrow Campground near Custer, South Dakota. I had my mare, Maple, and Diane had her little mule, Rosie. Now that led to some confusion at times because my name is Rosie, and the mule is also Rosie. Sometimes Diane would reprimand her mule with a sharp "ROSIE' and I would dutifully answer "what?" But it all worked out well. Diane and I spent an afternoon laying out all our camping gear, sleeping bags, tents, stoves, food, etc. sorting and distributing so we did not duplicate and end up carrying too much unnecessary weight. We would only carry what we would need on our one riding animal ... no pack horse, so no extra luxuries! Maple and Rosie were fit, willing and able. We were ready to hit the Centennial Trail.

Another friend, from eastern South Dakota, happened to be staying at the Broken Arrow Campground too, and we enlisted her aid to drop us off at the trailhead. Let me also plug Broken Arrow Campground, a very horse friendly place! People come from near and far to stay here. There are beautiful pull-through parking areas for big rigs, nice pens for horses, hay for purchase, wonderful bath facilities and nightly ice cream socials. I made the comment that I thought maybe this place was above my standards and Diane replied that she was glad to know that I had standards! We loved this place. They were very accommodating to us and allowed us to leave our rigs parked there in an out of the way place while we were off on our ride. How nice was that? Really nice folks and a 5-star place in my book!

We loaded up Maple, Rosie and all our gear and drove out to one of the Centennial Trail access points, at Legion Lake along Rt. 16A. Vickie and her friend, Brenda, from PA took pictures of us as we departed into the unknown wilderness. I say wilderness for almost immediately we rode into the Black Elk Wilderness area, a beautiful ride. We had set out at 9:30 am on a nice, clear, sunny day. It got pretty warm, but we were mostly in pine forest on the trail. We rode 7.3 miles to the Iron Creek Trailhead. We took a 30-minute lunch break and ate jerky, boiled eggs, peanut butter, nuts, and granola bars. The Black Elk Wilderness area is gorgeous. There are lots of rocks but, being from WV, nothing intimidated us. Beautiful views of the rock cliffs and mountains of the Black Hills. We stopped to take lots of pictures from atop the ridge where the trail runs. Only one small rattlesnake impeded our progress along a narrow place in the trail. We caved and took a detour, leaving the snake to be king of the rock! We met two riders coming south on horseback. They told us they had just come from Mt. Rushmore where you can tie up at a hitching rail and go get an ice cream cone at the store! Now that sounded like a treat on this warm day, so our pace increased. We could see George Washington's head from the trail! Wow! That was cool. However, the small side trail that leads to the monument was unmarked and we missed it! Dang. No ice cream for us this day. We rode on toward Big Pine trailhead, riding along a 2–3-mile rocky, hilly stretch. It started to sprinkle lightly, and we stopped so Diane could put her "saddle slicker" on to keep her saddle and packs dry. My poncho spread out over my packs. Diane dismounted and was unrolling her slicker when Rosie, the mule, decided to take things into her own hooves and took off running back south, from whence we had come today! The rascal! We were shocked and it took me a minute to realize that Rosie was not coming back, and I took off up the trail after her. Back through the bad rocks and uphill! Maple was carrying about 225 lbs with me and all our gear, so it was not easy going. Some of Diane's gear was getting strewn along the trail. Diane was following along behind on foot, and I would let her pick up her gear ... her saddle slicker, her horn bag, etc. At the top of a steep hill, Rosie stopped to catch her breath and she turned to look back at us ... and then took off again, galloping merrily along. We finally caught up with her on a steep switchback. She tried an evasive maneuver, but I managed to get Maple past her where I could block her progress. I dismounted and walked up to catch her. I told her that her Mom was really mad at her!! I led her back down through the rocks and we met Diane coming up the trail carrying the gear that had fallen off. That was all the excitement we needed for today. Whew. It was getting late in the day. We figured that we had done an extra 2-3 miles on this escapade.

We came to a paved road crossing where there were some houses and cabins. I filled our water bottles from an outside spigot at one house. We lost the Centennial Trail markers! The trail is marked with stakes that read RT. 89 and we could not find where the trail continued after it crossed the road. So, we headed right/east on the narrow-paved road. There was a railroad track right alongside the road and as the road curved, we crossed the straight track several times. We asked some people in cars if they knew where this road led and since most everyone around here at this time of year is a tourist, they could not tell us. We later learned that this road would take us to Keystone! Yikes. We probably rode an extra 4 miles on this mistake. We turned back and by riding along the railroad track near where we had first come to the road, we found the RT. 89 marker! That always makes us feel stupid! Our fault entirely. We met two more folks on horseback coming south and they told us that we were just about to come to a nice clover field with a creek where we could camp. Yea. We rode on and found that beautiful spot. Maple and Rosie thought this was heaven and dove into the clover with zest. Yummy. We were high lining our steeds at night, and I had left

Maple's tie line long so that she could graze on the clover beneath the high line while I set up our tent and got supper underway. Rosie is very good about being tied long and grazing without getting tangled, but, alas, Maple got her rope between her legs (front and back) and started bucking as the rope was "goosing" her!! Yikes. What a rodeo. I dashed over and pulled my quick release knot which freed her. She immediately stopped the bucking, but the damage was done to her muscles between her chubby hind legs. They were shredded with skin peeling off in sheets. Dang. There was no access for the horses to get to the creek, so we were using our collapsible buckets for water. I used my bush rag (neckerchief) and cold water from the bucket to soak, bath, and sooth the rope burns. It was painful but Maple stood stoically while I washed her wounds. She was shaking with fear and probably pain, so I gave her some bute (a good horse analgesic) tabs. It was now almost dark as Diane, and I sat down to our spaghetti dinner and raspberry cobbler. I put bacitracin on Maple's burns before crawling into bed. I fell asleep not knowing if our ride would be over come morning. I slept well but was worried about Maple.

We got up at 5 am when nature called. We are both early risers anyway and these days were too beautiful to waste. We grazed the girls and Maple was fine! Yea. She gobbled up clover like there was no tomorrow. She is a tough cookie and I love her! I was amazed. We had oatmeal and tea for breakfast and we were feeding the girls a little grain twice/day which they loved. It took us a while to get packed and loaded but we got better and faster at it. We rode out at 8:15 am. We came to the feared/famous tunnel after just a couple of miles. We had to get off an lead through it as it is only 7 feet high and 4 feet wide. No problem. It took us under the Rt. 16 highway. I should mention that Diane and I both ride in Sports Saddles, which are not really made for packing, so our saddlebags, packs, sleeping bags, etc are mostly just tied on as best we can get them. Diane's packs rode better than mine, but I had covered lots of miles with Maple all loaded and things went well as long as I was sitting in my saddle to keep things balanced. It was when I was leading her that the problems arose ... the saddle and packs would slip on Maple's chubby frame! At one point I got off to let us through a gate and not looking back at Maple while leading her along the trail a few feet, I was dismayed to see that my saddle and packs had slipped and were now under Maple's belly! She never panics when this happens, and it has happened before (on my Sandhills ride!)! We had to stop, and I had to remove everything, which is not easy when the saddle is under the horse! I was a bit angry having to pack up twice on this lovely morning. Wasted time to me! I got everything reloaded and up the trail we went. We rode some gorgeous trail with 3 hard climbs in rocks along here, but the climbs are not long or steep. We passed the Samelius Trailhead and rode 7 miles to Sheridan Lake. We came down the trail to a gravel road and once again, lost the trail markers! It was pretty hot this day, 90 degrees and we rode up to a guy's house and asked for water. We had seen lots of horses in paddocks which gave us hope for getting water. The man was very nice and filled our water bottles with wonderful, cold water. We asked the man for directions to the Centennial Trail, and he directed us toward the Sheridan Lake campground. He was not a rider and as it turned out, he did not know the trail or that horses are not allowed in the campground! We rode about 2 miles to the campground and got turned away. A nice official lady at the campground directed us to roads that would take us around the campground. OK, we followed her directions, stopping for lunch in a nice, treed area, and found that she had directed us onto Rt. 385, a busy 2 lane highway with 65mph speed limit, 18 wheelers and lots of speeding cars! Yikes. This would not do. We turned back when we reached the highway. We rode back to where we had lost the trail and easily spotted the trail marker that we had not seen coming from the other direction. Yea. We were back in business. Our fault again. We were drinking a lot of water and I again filled our water bottles from a spigot at a house along the way. Again, we were kicking ourselves for going another 4 miles out of our way. We rode around Sheridan Lake where there were lots of people enjoying the lake with boats and jet skis. Maple did not like this part. The trail along the lake is beautiful though and we did enjoy it. We crossed beautiful Spring Creek where Maple and Rosie got a good drink. We passed Dakota Point and rode into some cow pastures and woodsy trails.

We made camp along a two-track dirt path beside a mostly dry cow creek with just a few puddles where dark brown (cow manure?) water lay. It was hot and humid, and we were able to get water for the girls from a couple of pooled spots. Diane demonstrated her perfectly wonderful water filter unit here! She filtered enough of the brown, dirty water for our needs! It was amazing to watch the dirty brown water come out crystal clear! We had plenty of water for our supper and breakfast meals. Another success story! We had eaten jerky, granola, nuts, and left over cobbler for lunch near Sheridan Lake so we had tuna and noodles for supper. At this camp, it was Rosie's turn to get caught in her tie rope! She is usually very good about not getting tangled and had been grazing on a long line everywhere we had tied up, but this time, the rope got around her right hind fetlock when she rolled and made a burn! Dang. More bute and bacitracin, along with Vaseline and tea tree oil. I was still treating Maple's burns that were now scabbing over.

Up at 5:15 am. We fed grain and grazed our steeds. We found them a puddle they liked. We had oatmeal and tea. We packed up and rode away at 8:30 am., under an overcast sky. It soon began to rain lightly, and we put our slickers/poncho on. We rode into some gorgeous country ... the bald hills areas, through open, hilly cow pastures. Wow, these cows sure had it nice. We found good water at the cow tanks that ran with delicious, cold, clear water.

The trail was a bit difficult to follow because the cows knock the Rt. 89 trail markers down! But we found our way and got back into beautiful pine forests and went around Pactola Reservoir which is fed from Rapid Creek. We met 3 mountain bike riders and had a nice visit with them. We are advocates of multiuse trails! We asked them about creeks, as we had not seen any water since the bald hills. No, they did not remember crossing any creeks ... well, duh, they had ridden across Rapid Creek on a footbridge, so did not remember any fords! We got to Rapid Creek ourselves and crossed a couple of narrow footbridges to the trailhead parking area. It was drizzling slightly, and we sat under the USFS outhouse porch to eat our lunch. The rain eventually stopped, and we rode on and stopped about 4 pm at a place with good clover for grazing but no creek or water source. There were lots of nice pine trees for our picket lines and we grazed the girls on the wet clover which satisfied them nicely. We had just enough people water to fix our lasagna and chocolate mouse for supper! And tea. I will say that the REI freeze dried meals were all delicious and make for light weight packing. Diane had brought all of these delicious meals and we did enjoy them. We gave bute to Maple and Rosie and doctored their burns. Maple's scabs were now prompting questions from folks we met along the trail! They were colorful. The sun broke out in the evening, and it was pleasantly cool after our first two hot days. I figured that we were camped about 2 miles south of Pilot Knob.

No rain in the night. Cool, low humidity. Maple and Rosie did well on their pickets, and we had a quiet night. Up at 6 am. We had oatmeal but skipped our tea for lack of water. We packed quickly after grazing the girls on the wet clover. They were fine. We rode out at 8 am after watching 2 red squirrels playing up and down the pine trees. We rode on to Pilot Knob and found a good creek there. We watered the girls there and Diane filtered lots of water for us. Nice USFS outhouse. We rode on to the Box Elder Creek trailhead, 7.6 miles ahead. This part of the Centennial Trail is open to 4 wheelers, and we saw 2 in the first hour, then 3 more, then 2 and another 2 at the end. All sensible and polite about sharing the trail. Not a problem for us. Pretty trail, a two track through here. We stopped for lunch in a field and were lucky to find some raspberries. Diane was having fruit withdrawal about now, so this was a lucky find. When we reached the Box Elder trailhead, we saw a group of riders on horseback and some 4 wheelers. We turned right as I was looking for civilization and maybe a store. We had reached Nemo, that we came to love! We turned into a horse rental/trail ride place to ask about a store and asked if our animals could get a drink from the trough there. A man came out and said that he thought our critters looked healthy and that we were welcome. Paul Dangle turned out to be one of the most wonderful people we had ever met! He was the owner of this riding stable and just the nicest guy! The sky was getting really dark, and it was quite obvious that a big storm was approaching. Paul pointed up the field to a small cabin and told us that we were welcome to stay there if we wanted. It looked like a 5-star hotel to us! We quickly unloaded our saddles and gear on the cabin porch and put our critters in a big round pen that Paul had made ready for us. He had his crew put hay and water in the pen for us! We felt like royalty! Paul had directed us to the little store, at the Nemo Guest Ranch, about ¼ mile up the road. We walked to the store after getting Rosie and Maple settled in the round pen. It is funny the things you crave when camping. I bought a tomato juice and Diane got a Pepsi! We got ice cream and candy! We stocked up on a few camp things like multigrain bars, trail mix and a can of fruit cocktail. Everyone was so very nice. Troy and Willie, owners of the Guest Ranch, welcomed us and said we could even use their phone if we wanted. We would do that later. Since Paul had said that we could stay the night, we went back to the little cabin and got our stuff organized. We got our gear inside none too soon ... the heavens opened! It poured hard with thunder and lightening for the next 3 hours! We were sure glad to be inside. The cool temp felt great. Maple and Rosie got a good bath! We read and rested. Then, after the stable crew got horses put away and pens cleaned ... did I mention that this was the cleanest rental stable that I had ever seen? ... we visited with the nice crew. Paul, Sam, Bren, and Steve, all made us feel very welcome. I had a cell signal here and I made a few phone calls trying to arrange for our pickup when we reached the north end of the trail some 90 miles from our trailers. Sam, Bren, and Steve were soaked from being caught out in the rain with riders! They told us that they were taking us to supper with them! This was turning into a party! We piled into 3 vehicles and drove about 20 miles to Mystic Hills Resort where there is a wonderful restaurant/bar. This was Saturday night, and the place became packed. There was a nice, roaring fire going in the big stone fireplace and that helped warm the chilled Sam, Bren, and Steve whose clothes were steaming. We enjoyed prime rib dinners with baked potato, salad, and rolls. All yummy. Diane and I whispered to each other that we were going to treat the lot for being so nice to us but when we snuck up to pay the bill, Paul had already taken care of it and would not take anything! We were humbled. We left a generous tip for the friendly waitress that knew the stable folks. We were driven home in a thick fog and had dessert in the office at the stable. Cosco brownies and fresh oranges. What a fun day this was. We were getting to know these folks well and had a nice visit with them. Paul gave us a flashlight to take to the cabin.

There was a small electric heater in the cabin too. It was damp and chilly, a dark and stormy night. We were cozy. Diane crawled into the top bunk at 9 pm and fell right to sleep. I read for a little while and then slept like the dead too. Better than a Holiday Inn!

We got up about 6 am to check on Maple and Rosie. They were fine, all washed off! We used the outhouse and then sought out Paul to buy some more hay. There was a 7:30 am trail ride going out so we knew we could find someone early. Paul would not take any money for the hay but Diane stuffed some money in his shirt anyway! We fed the girls and guessed that it was about 40 degrees! The trail ride went out with Steve. A nice Father and son from Florida … this was the tourist season. We took Paul to breakfast at the Nemo Guest Ranch café. At least he let us do that! We enjoyed a delicious breakfast (my favorite meal) of eggs, bacon toast and tea. We even asked the kitchen if they would boil 6 eggs for us to take with us! They did. Nemo is a fun place.

There are old buildings there from the 1800's, an old barn, and an old, covered wagon. Box Elder creek runs right through the old town. The Guest Ranch also has covered horse pens for $10/night. All in all, Nemo was a gold mine for us! There were lots of guests staying in the cabins there. They do a lot of family reunions and weddings. We even saw a bride in a beautiful dress!

We packed up and rode out at noon! It was a beautiful day, sunny and clear. Paul had taken a group of riders out and we ran into him on the trail as we left. We thanked him all over the place and agreed that we would be sending him a donation for his hospitality. Rosie was a little sore from her rope burn, so we stopped on the trail and gave her some bute. We made our way slowly north on a very rocky trail with several steep climbs. Diane led Rosie a lot today. Since Maple walks about 1 mph, Diane had no trouble keeping up! After we climbed and got to the ridge, the trail and views were drop dead gorgeous! Wow. This is pretty country! We only did 6.5 miles today which was fine after our lazy/late start, hard climbs, and sore limbs. We reached Dalton Lake at 3:30 pm and were glad to stop. We set up our camp just behind a nice USFS outhouse where there were lots of nice, tall pines for picketing and lush grass for grazing. We had tea and candy while Maple and Rosie grazed. We were still stuffed from our Nemo stop, so we did not even cook anything for supper! We ate a boiled egg, nuts, an orange, and yogurt covered pretzels. That satisfied us. There was no one around when we stopped but late in the day a lot of 4 wheelers pulled into the parking lot and had a long visit after their ride.

The 4-wheeler trail is separate from the horse trail coming into this trailhead.

This was a nice, secluded spot. There is a good creek from which we carried water as the access to it is through a people gate from the parking lot. I had to research the trail markers here as the Centennial Trail has been redirected here and the old markers would have taken us on the old route had we not talked to the camp host! He was interesting and first told us that we could be fined for camping here! Don said that we could not camp within 5 miles of the campground and no horses are allowed in the campground. This seemed impossible but Don said that he was not going to run us off. It was getting colder, and we needed to crawl into our tent immediately and not go stumbling around after dark trying to find and set up camp 5 miles away. We would take our chances! We had not even known that there was a campground up the road. As it was, we shivered all night because of not getting settled in the tent before it got too cold.

Up at 5 am when Don's lady friend drove around the parking lot honking her horn! A rude awakening. We got up and moved quickly to warm up. I boiled water for oatmeal and tea. We fed and grazed Maple and Rosie. They were fine and enjoying the cool temp. Don came by about 6:30 am to apologize for his girlfriend's behavior! Diane told Don that maybe he should rethink his options in this area! We packed up and rode out at 8 am. Diane had said that she would open all gates today and had no idea what that would mean! The rerouted trail goes up a steep, forested hill in a series of switchbacks with a 3-foot wide, metal gate at each turn! Diane had to open 6 gates in the first 2-3 miles! Our packs barely fit through the narrow gates and we wondered who or why such narrow gates were placed here. Barbed wire on the posts tore a small rip in my sleeping pad. Rosie was feeling great today and she led all day. Maple seemed a bit lazy today. We rode up and down in gorgeous hill country with huge rocks (the size of houses) and bluffs. I had to stop for pictures of course. We came to Elk Creek at noon where Maple and Rosie drank a lot. We stopped for lunch right on the narrow trail where the girls nibbled on leaves while we ate jerky, boiled eggs, an orange, multigrain bars, pretzels, etc. We stopped for an hour. Diane filtered us each a good bottle of water from the creek. We rode on to the Elk Creek trailhead at 2 pm. We made good time with Rosie inspired and setting a good pace, normal for her. We rode east and west to go north around some canyons. Beautiful country. As it turned out, there is no creek or water at the trailhead! We met some really nice folks there, in a car, who were touring the area on the back roads. They were having a tailgate party and eating their lunch. They offered us food! Diane readily accepted the offer of fresh veggies and fruit! They gave us bottles of spring water too. I asked them if they had seen any water around and they said yes, they had driven past a spring just down the road. Then, they offered to drive me down to it, which was a good thing because it was more than a couple of miles down the road! We got water in their picnic coolers and brought it back to the trailhead. I laid out my ponchos between some large rocks and we had a water trough! That was so nice of those folks to help us out. As it turned out, we began talking to them about where they were from (eastern SD) and they knew our friend

Vickie (also from eastern SD) who had dropped us off at the start of this adventure! Small world. One of the gals got stung by a bee about then and Diane used some of her holistic pain ointment that she had obtained in Nemo which gave the gal immediate relief! We chatted with them quite a while before they drove away, leaving us with food and water! Diane was revived on the fresh veggies and fruit! We set up our camp on a slope and picketed the critters. We grazed the girls on the sparse grass, and they were fine. We ate our last freeze-dried dinner here: oriental chicken/rice/veggies. We also ate pistachios, an orange, candy, and tea. When the sun went down behind the mountain, it cooled off quickly. We crawled in the tent with all our clothes on (day clothes and night clothes!) for warmth. Another chilly night.

Up at 5 am. Again, we moved swiftly to warm up. Diane gave Rosie bute again. I had given Maple some last evening, as she seemed a little foot sore. We grazed the girls to warm them up. Rosie was shivering. We had oatmeal and tea and the girls gobbled up their grain. As the sun broke over the hill (slowly), it began to warm up. We hit the trail at 8:20 am. A beautiful day and a beautiful trail! We were loving every inch of this! Maple and Rosie grazed along the way as we rode across areas where pine slash had been plied up for winter burning.

The piles looked like hundreds of teepees across the fields. We came to a creek at 11 am. We met a lady on a big quarter horse gelding. She lives nearby and rides these trails a lot. She was interested in our trip! We were getting close to I-90 (yuk) and civilization. Diane and I both love it when no phones or cars are near. We stopped for lunch high atop a ridge covered with tall pines. We sat on the pine needle carpet and ate pepperoni sticks, peanut butter, jerky, trail mix, and candy. Diane and I are both chocoholics and like to end a meal with something chocolate! We rode on down the ridge, crossed under I-90 through a tunnel. We did not enjoy hearing the busy traffic! We got cell service (sort of), and I started locating someone to haul us back to Custer. We rode into the Alkali Creek campground, the horse camp, and set up camp. We called a friend who lived near Sturgis, and she came out to visit us after she got off work! Kerry brought her Mom, Millie, along and what a delight she is. 87 years old and still riding her little mule on these trails! She and Diane were like soul mates! Taking advantage of the phone service and civilization (Sturgis was only 3 miles away), I ordered a pizza to be delivered! What a hoot! The nice camp host came to meet us, and she brought Diane fresh salad and cantalope which endeared her to us! I enjoyed pizza! We shared everything. The good news was that Kerry had brought us grain and weed free hay (required here) which was really nice. She knows this campground and the hosts very well, as she puts on an endurance ride here, so she told us that since we were the only folks here, we could just let Maple and Rosie loose to graze and drink because the campground is completely fenced! Wow, Maple, and Rosie loved that. They ran, rolled, and ate nonstop!

We sat under a pavilion and visited with Kerry and Millie for quite a while. We made our arrangements for the final 8 miles to Bear Butte, at the north terminus of the Centennial Trail. Kerry, Millie, and family would ride with us day after tomorrow. They love to ride, know this trail and were happy to show us the way. We had never met Kerry before, but she is the kind of person that you feel like you've known all your life after 10 minutes of chat! Kerry had to work the next day and our girls needed a day off, so we would rest here at the camp for a day and then finish the ride the next day. I think Maple and Rosie loved that plan! We pitched our tent near a picket line (there are permanent ones at this horse camp) and fell asleep enjoying the sounds of our girls munching the good hay from Kerry. We were all happy. There are nice outhouses here and a good water trough and potable water. We did our cooking under the pavilion and kind of got spread out on the picnic tables there. What a nice place to stay.

That next day was a bit stormy and windy, so it was good that we had not planned to ride that day. I hung up the fly sheet as a wind break at one end of the pavilion! Several people came in that day ... another endurance friend came to visit, a gal from BLM came by and a guy from BLM came and sprayed a wasp nest under the eve of the pavilion! We ate ramen soup for lunch. The camp host arrived with wonderful goodies: carrots, celery, tomatoes, cantalope and fresh mint for tea! Helen was spoiling us, and we appreciated it all! A big horse trailer rig pulled in and after visiting with us a bit and looking over maps, they were not going to stay here as this was not where they had hoped to ride. However, they forced some corn on the cob on us and a banana! Everyone was so darned nice. They were headed to Ten Sleep, WY to ride. We read, napped, talked, and made a few phone calls (from the camp host's phone). We counted 7 thunderstorms that came by that day. Our timing had been perfect on the whole trip! The camp host told us that it had probably been in the 30's last night when we were at Elk Creek! Yikes. We enjoyed chicken and rice with corn on the cob for supper! Diane was saved with the salads and fruit!

This turned out to be a perfect night. We both slept really well this night beneath the huge oak trees.

Up at 5:30 am. Windy, but not too cold. Diane gave the girls some hay. After their grain, we let them loose again. They headed out to the front part of the fenced area in search of the early sun. We heated water for oatmeal and tea. Cantalope. We began to pack up and got ready to ride. This would be a different kind of day for us. We would not carry our packs but would put them in Kerry's horse trailer. We first caravaned 2 trailers up to Bear Butte, our destination, and then returned to Alkali Creek campground to start our ride. Kerry, Millie, Colleen (Kerry's sister), Rick (Colleen's husband ... the man who had made the wonderful weed free hay that we had been enjoying), and 2 granddaughters arrived with their mounts. We off loaded their horses and Buck, Millie's little mule and then took the trailers to Bear Butte. Rick drove us back in a car and then, he did not get to ride with us ... he had to go make hay while the sun shone! We mounted up and set out on our last leg of the Centennial Trail.

Kerry, our Savior, knows this trail well and she led us out and up into the pines on a nice trail, Rt. 89, the Centennial Trail. After about 4 miles, we broke out on the plains and really felt the wind! It was beautiful country. We rode through Fort Meade, an old remount station like Fort Robinson in Nebraska. The red brick horse barns were a work of art when they were built around 1900 and they are still in excellent condition. We rode past the arsenal (yikes) and crossed the busy highway through another tunnel where we had to lead our mounts. Kerry is a high energy person and she got most all the gates for us that day. Her Mom, Millie, is a hoot riding her little mule, Buck! Millie had worked at Fort Meade for 35 years while raising her family near here. And Kerry's sister, Colleen, worked as a nurse at the post hospital for 31 years. This place has their names on it! They should name a wing after this nice family! We leaned into the wind as we topped the hill and rode across a ridge from where we had a great view of Bear Butte and a reservoir at its base. We could see the trailers that we had parked there earlier today. We took lots of pictures and Diane and I got a little quiet seeing that this was the end of our adventure. We had Kerry take our picture at the base of Bear Butte. It is possible to hike up the butte, but we did not have time to do that today and it would have been a challenge in the wind! There were antelope and cattle on the plains surrounding the butte. It had taken us about 4 hours to complete our ride and we enjoyed the wonderful company to the end.

Postscript: Kerry graciously drove us back to Custer and we laughed out loud at the fact that it had taken us 8 days to ride from Custer to Bear Butte and only 1.5 hours for Kerry to drive us back to our start! Too funny! We all enjoyed a great supper to celebrate our ride and then bade goodbye to our new friends.

The day after we returned to our starting camp, we hauled out to the Badger Hole Trailhead and rode the Centennial Trail south to the French Creek Trailhead and Horse Camp. Wow, that is a nice spot ... complete with roaming, wild buffalo and a nearby ice cream store! Since we were not overnight or camping this day, we did not carry any packs. As it turned out, this was a very good thing ... yikes ... this part of the trail has some really, really rocky, steep, and narrow places on it. We would not have fit through some of the places if we had had our packs! But it was scenic, and we were glad to have ridden it and add another 10 miles to our total. We had not planned on riding on south into Wind Cave National Park and on the last 6 miles of the Centennial Trail. Those miles will call me back some other time. Meanwhile, I can treasure all the fond memories of the beautiful Centennial Trail and the time spent enjoying it.

100 MILE RIDES: THE TEVIS & THE OLD DOMINION

Dixie on Zack, Lynn on Chagall and Rosie on Blu crossing the Shenandoah River in Virginia (courtesy of Genie Stewart-Spears Photography)

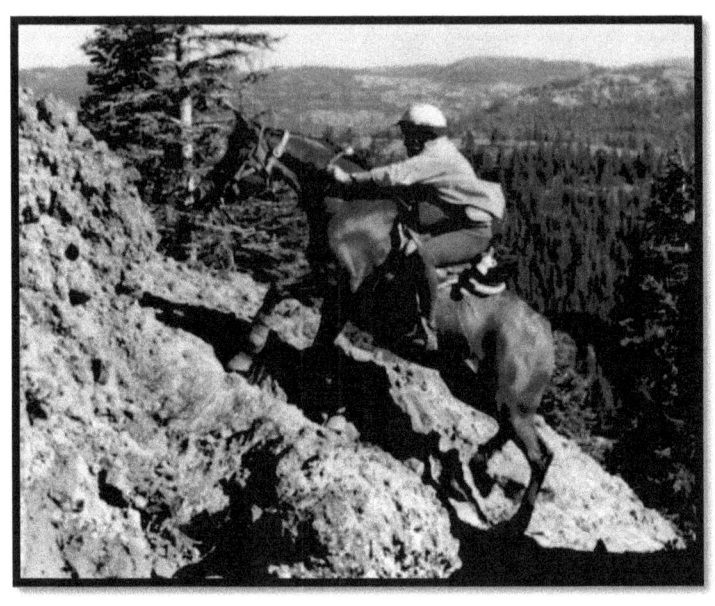

Rosie on Blu on Cougar Rock in California
(courtesy of Hughes Photography)

This was written in 2000 when the Tevis was in its 46th year and the Old Dominion was in its 27th year.

In the world of endurance racing, there are two premier 100-mile rides in the United States. California has the Tevis and Virginia has the Old Dominion.

The ride in California is officially called The Western States Trail Ride (WSTR), but it is affectionately known simply as "The Tevis." The first place trophy is named after Lloyd Tevis, president of Wells Fargo & Co. from 1872 to 1892. He went to California by covered wagon in 1849 and started a transportation company that moved freight and people across the country. His horses, coaches and express riders traveled parts or all of what would become the historical Western States trail through the difficult Sierra Nevada range and down to the foothills of California. It was the ill-fated Donner party that got stuck in these mountains in 1846 and only 49 of 91 emigrants made it out of the mountains! Today, this is a 100 mile-one day (24 hours) ride on a horse. Not for the fainthearted! In 1955, a man named Wendell Robie bet some friends that he could ride his horse from near lake Tahoe to Auburn, CA in less than 24 hours....a crazy bet his friends must have thought! He started the Western States 100 Mile-One Day ride in California. He completed this ride, held annually, 13 times and won it 4 times, an enviable record! It is not an easy task, ask anyone who has tried it: over 46 years some 7000 riders have attempted it and only about 2000 have completed it.

So, California has its Tevis and Virginia has the Old Dominion one day ride. In the early 1970's, Alex Bigler, who had ridden the Tevis, moved to Virginia, and got the idea to start a one day-100-mile ride in Virginia. After 4 enthusiastic riders from the east took their horses out to the Tevis in 1973, the idea of starting a ride in Virginia took shape and brought Alex Bigler's dream to reality. A small committee was formed and made it happen. The ride was called The Old Dominion and it was held in Leesburg Virginia for its first 7 years and then was moved out to the Shenandoah Valley of Virginia, due to encroaching development and more and more roads. So, moving the ride out to the valley where the George Washington National Forest with its wonderful trails were seemed the solution. This year [2000], will be the 27th running of the Old Dominion Ride. The ride is actually a race, and the competitors are tested on a 100-mile trail. California has its pioneer history, but Virginia has a much older history as the east coast is where the US got its start. When the riders cross the Shenandoah River at McCoy's Ford, it is a thrilling moment, both feared and revered by riders. There are few safe places to ford the Shenandoah River and McCoy's was one of the crossings that was used during our Revolutionary and Civil Wars! The Tevis has its famous Cougar Rock climb and Old Dominion has the ¼ mile Shenandoah River ford. There is nothing to compare with crossing the river at night, under the full moon! Both are huge thrills for endurance riders.

Even though endurance rides are a race, the definition of endurance riding is "to finish is to win" and "the horse must be fit to continue" (assuring the well being of the horse) and every rider who does complete the Tevis and Old Dominion earns a coveted silver buckle. This sport has excellent and meaningful criteria for a sport. The rides are veterinary controlled and both rides assemble a huge team of experienced veterinarians to carefully monitor the horses throughout the ride.

So how long does it take to ride a horse 100 miles in under 24 hours through the mountains? It has been done in under 12 hours of riding time! Think about that pace on your next drive to work! The public knows little about this sport because it is not particularly a spectator sport since it takes place over 100 miles of trail in remote forests. Support vehicles are able to meet horses and riders at a few points along the trail. Veterinary stops are designated and mandatory. These "vet checks" are places where pit crews can meet their rider and lend support in the way of food, drink, dry clothes, etc. Sometimes the horse needs a new pair of shoes along the way and a farrier is available at certain points.

The Old Dominion is held annually the 2nd Saturday in June and the Tevis is held on a Saturday nearest to a full moon in either July or August. Those who participate in this sport treasure the moments on the trail for it is a special relationship between man and horse for many hours and the ones with the best bond seem to have an advantage. There are times when it seems magical and mystical to be out there in the sun, rain, fog, dark of night with your best friend, both lives in each other's hands/hooves.

THE PERFECT CAMP
AKA CAMPING WITH BERNICE

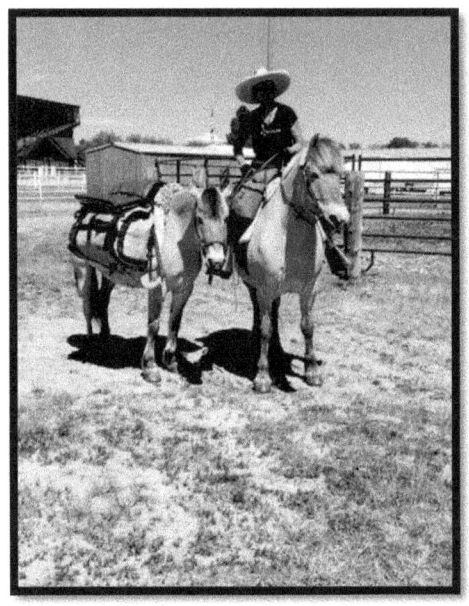

TREGO the sign read. Wait...what? That is where Bernice Ende lived! I must stop and see if I can locate her. My dog, Bella, and I were on our way back from a driving trip to the Yukon. I crossed back into the USA at the Roosville border crossing and headed south in Montana. That is when I saw the road sign for Trego. Now I had been following Bernice Ende's blog on the internet for several years, longing to make the long rides on horseback as she did.

What is a long rider? Someone who rides a horse 1000 miles without vehicle or trailer assistance. The rider must be self sufficient, camping out and getting necessary supplies on her own. Bernice had raised the bar on long riding by riding her horses more than 30,000 miles in the USA and Canada.

I had done what I called "short, long rides" myself and really admired Bernice's rides. My rides were just a few 100 miles long, whereas Bernice had enjoyed days, weeks, months, and years on the roads. I was envious. So, I pulled into Trego on a mission. Of course, I did not know if Bernice would even be at her home in Montana at this time, but I would give it a go to find her. Trego consisted of two buildings: a US Post Office and a bar/grocery store! I pulled in after 4 pm and the PO was closed for the day. I went into the small mini mart store and asked the young clerk if he knew Bernice Ende. He had heard of her but did not know her. He tried looking her up on his computer, looking for a phone number or something, but had no luck. I went into the adjoining bar where there were several men having an adult beverage. They were very friendly and offered to buy me a drink. I asked if they knew Bernice. YES! But whether they were trying to protect her or just did not trust me, I did not know, but one of them told me that I did not want to go up her road as it was not for the fainthearted. They underestimated me! I thanked them and returned to my truck where Bella waited. Just as I was about to pull out, a gal rode in on her 4-wheeler with her German shepherd dog following. She looked like one of us! Jeans, muddy boots, sweatshirt, and the rugged outdoor look of a horsewoman. I asked her if she knew Bernice. YES! After I introduced myself and told her that I had followed Bernice's blog for years and was a kind of long rider myself, she warmed up to me and said that she not only knows Bernice but rides horses with her sometimes. WOW! She gave me directions to Bernice's place, about 8-10 miles out of town. Only the last mile, which was the driveway, was a bit muddy with a few potholes. So, Bella and I headed that way.

I drove up to a barbed wire gate and stopped. I saw a man walking about and he came down to the gate to see what I wanted. I told him that I was looking for Bernice as I was an admirer. I was wondering who he was? Then I heard a woman's voice shout out "Who is it?" I shouted out that I was "Rosie, a short, long rider!" She wondered what that meant and shouted to "Come on up." The man opened and closed the wire gate for me. The voice was that of Bernice Ende! I had found her. What an honor! She was seated on the porch of her off the grid log home. She invited me to join her and offered me a cool glass of water, telling me that her water flows downhill from a spring farther up the mountain. We sat on the porch and got acquainted. I gave Bernice a copy of my recently published book, Adventures On Horseback. I think she looked at me a bit differently now. She asked me to autograph it for her. I did. Then, she told me that she would give me a copy of her book when it finally gets published. I knew that would be a great read. BTW, the man who had opened the gate for me was Burton, a long-time admirer of Bernice whom she had met on one of her rides across Michigan where he lived.

Burton came to be one of my dear texting friends! He always wanted to live in Montana, but his wife did not, so he just took his husky dog and his camper to stay at Bernice's from time to time and then returned home to his wife.

Bernice's book was to come out soon, but I knew how that process went and it takes time to come down the home stretch. She turned to me and asked me if I would like to take her on her book tour if and when the book came out. I was in awe. Bernice now knew that I had a nice rig and lots of experience hauling horses around the country, and I had mentioned that I had intended to spend some winter months in the southwest, riding and exploring Arizona and New Mexico trails. That got her interest. We then walked out into the field where her two Fjord mares were grazing. Huge Ponderosa pines dotted the small field. The horses came right up to us for a pat. Bernice said that it was time to put them in the barn for the night as this was grizzly country and she always had to be vigilant. The mares followed us to the big open barn. She had to keep the mares in separate pens because.....they were mares! She left them with hay and water, and we returned to the porch to lay some plans. In Bernice's mind it was a done deal. I was not so sure, but we talked it out. Bernice did not own a vehicle or trailer at the time. Her horses were her transportation. We exchanged phone numbers. She invited me to stay the night, but I felt that I needed to continue south towards Nebraska where my horse was waiting. A book tour? Her book was not out yet. Bernice's mares were Spirit and Liska. Spirit was tall for a Fjord and Liska was small for a Fjord. Bernice had just acquired Liska that spring and was in the process of training her for the life of long riding, getting used to packs and ponying, Spirit was already a seasoned long riding horse. Nothing bothered her! Bernice told me that when Liska came off the trailer that delivered her, Bernice wept....not tears of joy but tears of shock at how small and neglected the little mare was. Bernice began remaking little Liska. Attitude and horse hooves being the most important. Bernice had a way with horses for sure. The little mare began bonding to Bernice and Spirit. Bernice worked on her feet and nutrition for her coat. Slowly, the little horse came around and Bernice named her Liska Pearl. Spirit was laid back and would take care of herself and Bernice without question. I came to love both of them later that year.

I had not driven 10 miles down the road when my cell phone rang. It was Bernice, I think testing our phones to see if we could stay in contact. She was excited about our traveling together this winter. We had laid some vague plans about meeting up in November and heading south for the winter. Summer and fall passed, and I had a death in my family that resulted in me putting my TN house up for sale. My plans for wintering in the southwest were something to look forward to. Bernice called from time to time to keep me apprised on Liska's progress and our plans to meet in November.

I had been in Nebraska in early October house/horse/dog/cat sitting for my friends when I got word of a death in my family. I zoomed back to Virginia to be with family. The last week of October I returned to

Nebraska to begin my adventures with Bernice. She called me and said, "I'm ready to be picked up."!!! In Montana? I told her that was not going to happen as I was not driving 1500 miles to pick her up. She said she would make her way down to southern Idaho where we could meet up. OK. As it turned out, Bernice had been busy since I had visited her in July. She had become the owner of a 1969 Ford pickup truck and a 12-foot stock trailer. A friend who had bought that truck new in 1969 had given her the truck just before his passing. She bought the used stock trailer to complete her rig! The problem she had to overcome was her fear of driving the rig with her precious horses in it. She was terrified. After all, her only transportation for the last several years had been her horses. She sucked it up and said that she would meet me at the fairgrounds in Montpelier Idaho around November 1 or 2. So I set out from Nebraska Nov. 1st.

It was almost 600 miles and Bella, and I took 2 days to get to Montpelier. Bernice and I had decided that I would leave my mare in her retirement splendor in Nebraska, and I would haul Spirit and Liska in my trailer. We only needed two horses. Our deal was that I would be responsible for the truck and trailer, and she would be responsible for the horses. We both felt good on that front. I arrived at the fairgrounds in Montpelier just as it began to snow. Bernice was there. It had taken her several days to drive from Trego to Montpelier as she could only do about 200 miles/day at 35 mph!

She said it was a white-knuckle experience! At the fairgrounds she had her tent pitched inside her stock trailer to be out of the elements. The old Ford truck was next to the trailer with snow accumulating on it. This was the first time I had seen Bernice's tent home. The horses were out grazing/foraging around the fairgrounds which they do well staying fat on weeds! I was glad that I had my comfy trailer to sleep in. So was Bella. The temperature was in the 20s! Bernice greeted me with enthusiasm and told me that we had a supper invitation that night in town. What? Bernice has made friends all over America so this did not really surprise me. We put the Fjords in stalls, covered supplies and I drove us to Elaine's house in downtown Montpelier Idaho. What a warm and fun night that turned out to be. First time I had ever had cauliflower crust pizza! There ended up being about 10 people around the little table with wonderful folks and plenty of good food. I think there was some wine involved too. The snow continued to fall outside. We returned to the fairgrounds well after dark. We each went to our own abode, me in my trailer and Bernice in her tent. The snow stopped at about 5 inches. It was a cold night. I was to learn that Bernice stayed warm and cozy in her cleverly designed tent. I had a propane heater in my trailer.

The next morning, we cleaned snow off our rigs and got supplies loaded on to my truck and trailer. We laughed because when Bernice did her first ride which was from her home in Montana to her sister's home in New Mexico, she only had one horse. She says that she thinks she walked about 80% of the way leading the horse. She only had some saddlebags for supplies. Later, as she became Lady Long Rider, she had two horses, one to ride and one to pack. She said she could take everything she needed with 2 horses. Now, having my rig was a completely new set up for her; she could take an unlimited amount of supplies. She had several Rubbermaid totes full of stuff loaded in the truck bed. We even had room for hay bales in bags to keep them dry. And, since my trailer is a 3-horse slant and we only had 2 horses, we had another whole stall in the trailer for even more supplies. The back seat of my truck belonged to Bella and had the dog hair to prove it! We were outfitted for sure with everything we needed. We had gotten directions on a beautiful way out of town, through a canyon that was magical with all the new and sparkling snow. There were no tracks ahead of us when we set out south. We decided that we would drive until the temperature got above 50 degrees! We did just that. Bernice left her rig with Elaine in Montpelier.

We made our way south and stopped at the fairgrounds in Spanish Forks UT for a stretch. We cleaned out the trailer, filled water jugs, let the horses have a good run and roll in the arena and stretched our legs. Let me add that Bernice and I were both followers of the Leave No Trace mantra. We always left places cleaner than when we arrived! We loaded up and headed SE on back roads. That is what we both liked. We could stop anywhere! We spent that night near Green River UT, just out in the middle of a huge open area with mountains all around. There were cattle pens there, but they were locked up, so Bernice just picketed the horses and set up her tent beside them. She prefers to stay right with her horses. They are a pack. For many of her long rides Bernice was accompanied by her dog, Claire. Followers will remember pictures of Claire riding on top of the pack horse. Bernice was falling in love with Bella now.

We crossed over into Colorado and went in search of the Delores River. At the BLM office in Delores, we got a map and found our way to the McPhee Reservoir arrea and the House Creek Campground. It was a way off the beaten path, but we were pleased as we ended up with having the entire place to ourselves. I guess not too many nuts are out camping in Colorado in November. As it turned out, the campground was sort of closed for the winter, but the rangers said we could stay there since no one else was around. Yea. Bernice pitched her tent, and I unhooked the trailer. We rode the Fjords around the beautiful reservoir through pinon pine, sagebrush, and junipers. We even had a working water hydrant and a pit toilet that was unlocked. It was chilly at night and a bit windy during the day. Bernice took this opportunity to put new shoes on Spirit. That gives her a workout! What do we do in our camps? We are both readers and I always have several books in my trailer. I drink tea and Bernice drinks coffee which we enjoy sitting in our chairs to enjoy the scenery and the sounds of nature. Bernice did not have a cell phone and I was pretty new to my iPhone so that was not a distraction for us. We relied on having internet at cafes to check mail and communicate with folks. We found some wonderful cafes in many little towns. Some with home baked muffins & cinnamon rolls! While Bernice worked on shoes,

I took a drive south to Cortez where there is a Walmart. I stocked up on the small propane tanks and some food supplies. The next day we moved to the Bradford Camp along the Delores River. That was very nice, to hear the river babbling along all night long. We took a trail ride that took us alongside the river for a long way. Beautiful country. Another perfect camp, all to ourselves. We like that because Bella can run loose, and the horses can graze freely. Every now and then, I like to stay somewhere that has a shower and a TV. So, the next night we stayed at a horse B&B. I stayed in the lovely apartment and enjoyed a nice shower and watched some TV. Bella stayed with Bernice, in her tent which was pitched right beside the fenced field with the Fjords. The proprietors were very nice, the woman being an artist of many talents. And I sure enjoyed the delicious breakfast that came with the deal. We packed up and moved on south, passing into New Mexico. We stopped in Gallup at a huge hay market and bought more hay. These bales that we got were 150 lbs! We continued south to Bernardo NM and stayed at the Kiva Horse Motel. Well, I stayed there, and Bernice stayed about 0.2 mile down the road in a big open desert field where the Fjords could forage as opposed to being in a pen at the motel where we would have to feed hay. She pitched her tent and I set up a large electric pen for the horses. Of course, I had to haul water to her. I had met the owner of the motel on a previous trip, and we hit it off, going riding together several times. I also learned that Bernice knew Diane from one of Bernice's stops through here years before. Small world!Diane was fine with me taking water to Bernice. Again. I enjoyed showers and laundry at Kiva while Bernice camped down the road. We had a nice surprise while here. Bernice's sister came for a visit! She is a horse person too and probably worried about Bernice when she was off on her long rides. MaryAnn lived in NM and came to see us for the day. I think she was glad to meet me and see that Bernice was in good hands. MaryAnn brought us a feast of a meal to celebrate Bernice's upcoming birthday. She even brought a pie! We feasted at Bernice's camp out in the desert. We had to watch out for prickly pear cactus! After two days at Bernardo, we went further south to the San Lorenzo Canyon, again, a little-known spot with very few people. The owner of Kiva had taken me riding there on a previous trip, so I knew where it was. We just pulled in and camped in the sand there. It is a national wildlife refuge and the huge red rock formations are stunning. Little caves and old ruins. Trees struggling to keep their leaves and suck up precious water. It is a BLM site which we loved. Sandstone cliffs, arches, and cottonwoods. All primitive camping which Bernice and I prefer. Some friends of mine hauled their horses in and we all did a day ride in the canyon. It is a good backdrop for photos! Those friends lived at Pie Town which was our next destination.

We packed up and drove west from Socorro towards Pie Town. This is the route of the Magdalena Trail, that was used from 1885 to the 1960s! Ranchers drove their cattle the 60 miles or so to the train depot at Magdalena. The drive took a week or so. Entire families went on the drive. Water wells had been dug every 10 miles so the stock would have water every night. They did about 10 miles/day and enjoyed the drive.

We passed by the VLA which is the Very Large Array, a long row of huge satellite dishes that are trying to make touch with outer space, I think. Each dish is 82 feet in diameter! It is the National Radio Astronomy Observatory and seems to go on forever across the land. Did you know that there are more backyard private observatories in NM than in any other state? It is because of their dark skies and open space. We rode the horses through a subdivision (Top of The World) where I saw lots of small observatories in backyards. We drove to a friend's place about 3 miles out of Pie Town. We camped there for a week. Another friend was living there in her RV, and we had all the comforts of home with TV, internet, and a place to cook full meals. We made Bernice fix supper for us one evening. The horses had a pasture to graze on. Thanksgiving was that week. The three of us rode our horses into Pie Town for the Thanksgiving service and dinner at the Baptist Church. The local children loved seeing the horses that we just tied to some trees behind the church while we went in to eat. There was enough scrumptious food to feed the masses that day and the whole town was there. I was only able to eat 4 desserts, I think! We were stuffed and wondered if the horses could feel the extra pounds on our way back home. It was a beautiful day and with wonderful, friendly local folks. One day that week Bernice and I hauled the Fjords to the Cibola National Forest and rode there enjoying views of the Sawtooth Mountains. We found a cow tank for water and lots of range cows. That was a very pleasant day ride. We also frequented Pie Town which is the place to eat fresh made pies of all kinds. People come from near and far to enjoy those pies. Hence the name, Pie Town.

We continued to make our way south and headed to Silver City New Mexico. I got Bernice and the Fjords settled in at the fairgounds. I unhooked my trailer there for her and she pitched her tent in the trailer because of the windy, inclement weather. Once her tent was pitched, Bernice was cozy and warm. I made a motel reservation in Silver City and spent one night there. Shower and TV. Bernice was in search of internet, and we got it at a MacDonald's. She was having to stay in touch with her publisher about her book. She was thinking on the cover picture and the title! You may be wondering how we made our plans about where to head next. Mostly it was word of mouth and depended a lot on friends of friends! The horse community never let me down. You have friends all over and most of them welcome you to stop in. Bernice and I never worried about where we were headed next. It all worked out. We bought some really nice hay in Silver City and then headed to the Gila National Forest. We camped at a trail head which was right next door to a horse friend's home! Annie used to be a cougar hunter as well as an endurance rider. An endurance rider is someone who races a horse on 25–100-mile rides! Call us crazy but we are a close-knit group. I knew Annie through my friend in Pie Town. Annie supplied us with water from her place and we camped at the trail head. We had the place to ourselves. A perfect Camp!

We loved camping in the Gila. We took day rides in the forest and took picnic lunches to enjoy. When we stopped for a picnic or rest, we would untack the horses to let them roll and be free to graze. We could always find water at a cow tank or puddle. We enjoyed some great suppers at Annie's just a short walk away. Have you ever had caribou tacos? Bonfires and sometimes wine. We drove into Silver City for supplies and had a couple of great breakfasts at small cafes (with internet). Laundry too. I took a day trip to see the Gila Cliff Dwellings. Very interesting. Push the way back button! I could have lived there! We attended the Back Country Horsemen's Christmas dinner on Dec. 3 in Pinos Altos. That was a huge turnout with a lot of fun horse people there. I met a lady who had ridden her horse on the entire Santa Fe Trail, a distance of about 800 miles. I was impressed! Oh, I longed to do these things. We stayed there in the Gila for 9 days. We met more people that shared our love of horses. We packed up and headed south again. We crossed into Arizona and met our Pie Town friend again at the Empire Ranch near Sonoita AZ. Jeanetta used to live near there and she knew the area well. She introduced us to the Las Cienegas National Conservation Area. This used to be all the Empire Ranch. Over 100,000 acres! Now it is BLM land with the Empire Ranch buildings being a foundation that preserves the history of the original ranch. The buildings date back to 1871. Walter Vail bought the ranch and its 612 head of cattle in 1876. At that time the ranch consisted of 160 acres. Vail would acquire and expand the ranch to over 100,000 acres. That is 180 square miles of land! Vails owned the ranch from 1876 to 1928. There would be 40,000 cattle on the ranch by 1898! In 1928 the ranch was sold to the Boice family who operated it until 1969. During the Boice ownership, many Hollywood movies were made there. Movies like 3:10 To Yuma, Desperado, Gunfight at the OK Corral, Duel in the Sun, Hour of the Gun, Hombre, Red River, The Cowboys and many more. The TV series Bonanza and Gunsmoke were made there. There is a lot of history to entertain you at the Empire Ranch. Eventually the ranch came to be owned by the BLM. Bernice and I followed Jeanetta into the property and to the airstrip where we camped. It is now used as a campground and there is a pit toilet and a water hydrant. A wide-open space and perfect for camping with horses and a dog. This is not near the original ranch buildings. They are on the National Register of Historic Buildings. Friends who lived nearby joined us there and we did some day rides through the dry washes and under the huge cottonwood trees, some 4 feet in diameter. Mark showed us the area on the ranch called Maternity Wells where there were cattle pens and lots of water tanks. We could see that a storm was brewing, and we felt a few beginning sprinkles. Uh oh. The next morning, we loaded up and moved to the Sonoita Fairgrounds a few miles south. We put the horses in stalls and went to eat at the Velvet Elvis in Patagonia. We were planning to ride from Patagonia in the future. We ran into an open-air market where Bernice bought herself fruits and I stocked up on candy! An author was set up there selling her books, but I was more interested in her Anatole puppies! Boy, are they fuzzy and happy. We returned to the fairgrounds where Bernice had set up her tent in the horse trailer to be out of the wind and rain. We could take showers in the jockey room (nothing fancy). It was 25 degrees at night here. We only spent the one night and then moved our rig to Maternity Wells in the Cienegas. That turned out to be another perfect camp! We stayed on there for 6 days. We took trail rides or Bernice would take the Fjords for a bareback gallop.

While camped there, my birthday needed celebrating. I left Bernice and Bella at Maternity Wells and drove over to Sierra Vista, home of Fort Huachuca which was established in 1877. It is only 15 miles from the Mexican border. Sierra Vista is a busy Military town surrounded by AZ mountains like the Whetstones and the Mustangs. I treated myself to a great birthday supper at an Olive Garden and then took a motel room for the night. A shower and TV! Bernice gifted me a dvd of one of her tv interviews, a very nice gift indeed. I said that she had a lot of stuff packed into those Rubbermaid containers!

I returned to our Maternity Wells camp where we were greeted by a cool herd of antelope almost daily. They have it pretty good here with grass and water. Bernice and I took some day rides from camp with me feeling like I was in a western movie with John Wayne. We moved our camp up to the cattle pens which are closer to the ranch buildings. We did tour the buildings. It was going to storm again so Bernice had her tent in the trailer again and the horses were in pens beside us. They had lots of weeds to forage on. It was dang chilly at that time. And it got pretty windy. We rode the horses to the ranch buildings and met the gal who was managing the foundation. I made a contribution. A good cause in my mind. Sometimes I rode little Liska and sometimes I rode Spirit. I rode in a saddle while Bernice mostly rode bareback with just a sheepskin pad. Our rides were always fun. The next day the rains came with a vengeance. We loaded up and made a dash back to the fairgrounds. Horses in stalls, out of the wind and cold rain. Bernice and I went out to eat where we had WiFi and caught up on our emls. The next morning, we packed up, bought hay at the nearby feed store (120 lb bales) and drove west to Tubac, AZ. We did stop at Patagonia for a trail ride.

We stayed at a Horse B&B where Bernice pitched her tent next to the pen where her horses stayed. I stay in my trailer, my home away from home. We both feel like we have everything we need. One of Bernice's fans came to visit her here and they got in a nice story time about long riding. The gal had ridden her mule from AZ to TX and yearned to do more long riding. Fans yearn to get tips from Bernice on how to do these long rides. Bernice and I wanted to see a special exhibit in Tubac, at the Presidio, a State Historic Park. We walked about, had lunch, and found the exhibit which was Lady Bronc Riders. Lots of names, photographs, and outfits from the pioneering women. Bernice admired strong women who forge ahead in life. Some of these tough bronc riders died doing what they loved and then, men took that opportunity to ban women from bronc riding for the next 50 years. It was a very interesting and well-done exhibit. We toured the mission at Tumacocori, and I still marvel at how they built such massive structures without all the machines that we use today. We stayed another night at the B&B Motel. Ice on the water in the morning.

We packed up and drove north towards Tucson. We stopped at a Walmart in Saharita and did our odd shopping. Bernice with goodies for the horses and me with junk food! We drove on the the Oro Valley and pulled into the Catalina State Park where there is a nice Equestrian camping area. Very nice pens and wheelbarrows to clean trailers and pens. Remember, Leave No Trace. Bernice went riding with some local gals who pulled into day ride while I took my rig to get some maintenance done: a new tire for the trailer and an oil change for the truck. While I was out, I met up with a dear friend who lives in Tucson, and we did lunch! Then, back to camp for another night in the desert air. Pleasant. It could have been another perfect camp if there were not so many people around.

The next morning, we loaded up and drove to Apache Junction, a favorite winter camping spot for horse owners. There are many horse facilities, private campgrounds there. Bernice had been contacted by a gal/fan, Melissa, who had arranged for Bernice to give a talk. Now this is something that Bernice had been doing on her long rides for years. It would give her some pocket money and it was fun and interesting to her listeners. Her talks are very entertaining as she tells of her perils and fun on the road. Her upcoming book would tell a lot of her stories and adventures. These winter horse camps are way too crowded for Bernice and me, so we drove east to Superior AZ and pulled off at Picketpost

Mountain where we had pens, water, and the whole place to ourselves. A perfect camp! We met the camp host at the Picketpost Trail Head, where the Arizona Trail (AZT) passes, but no overnight camping was allowed there, so we just pulled off and found our own great spot about 2 miles away. We rode bits and pieces of the AZT in both directions. It is amazing to me how we could come upon green grass and small bits of water while riding this desert! I think it is beautiful country. Nice daytime temperatures and a wee bit nippy at night. We remained here through Christmas.

We attended Christmas eve service at a Spanish Presbyterian Church in Superior AZ while we were camped at Picketpost. What did we do on rainy/windy days? We were both readers and writers. Bernice would write on her laptop in her tent, and I would do my reading and writing in the dressing room of my trailer. Sometimes we would both sit in the trailer (for the heater) and have a tea or wine. We shared some personal stories too. We both had loved and lost. Neither of us had a child. We each had our own careers. She loved her years of teaching ballet and she certainly stayed in shape by exercising and working out. We would both read the same book and then had our own little book club discussions. We would talk about book titles and covers. We talked about many of her friends that she had met on her travels. We both loved riding horses. Here is a little-known fact: Bernice did not like riding trails! She rode roads! She asked me what was the point of trail riding which astonished me. Of course, the answer was spending time with my horse and enjoying nature. All her riding was with purpose and with a destination in mind. Her Mother had told her to search for the horizon, and she did just that. She always had a goal and went about attaining it by studying the map. I enjoyed hearing some of her stories that she did not include in her book. Broken bones, starvation and worry often dominated her days. She mostly rode roads but also had to go cross country at times. Over mountain passes clogged with snow or holing up in roofless cabins out of the wind. She depended a lot on the kindness of strangers who then became friends of Lady Long Rider. She was to be admired. Bernice suffered from alopecia and told me that for years that held her back. You may recall that her large hat was a symbol for her. She had found her stride and rode with it!

We drove into Apache Junction to pick up Bernice's mail that a friend had been collecting for her. She had a friend managing her website: Ende of The Trail which I thought was very clever! That was where she posted her blogs and let folks know where she was. Mostly she kept to herself while gathering experience along the way. We did a few days north of Superior camping beside Lake Roosevelt. There was a new Equestrian campground there. Bernice took the horses swimming in the lake! We went to see the nearby cliff dwellings. Bernice put new shoes on Spirit while we were camped at the lake. We moved back to Picketpost for New Years! We had our own campfire after attending a potluck at the Arboretum (which is worth a look for sure). We listened to Auld Lang Syne on the little radio and watched our fire die out. To our beds. We awakened to the new year, 2018. I attended the smoke blessing by the Native Americans at the Arboretum. Arvel Bird played the flute and the fiddle to welcome the new year. We watched the rising of the full, super moon that night. A perfect camp! That night we had potatoes and veggies cooked in foil in our bonfire. Yummy. Neither of us was a late-night party fly; usually off to our beds by 8 pm! Nights are long during the winter months!

On January 2 we went into Superior for a restaurant meal and WiFi.

A hunter came by in the afternoon and gave us 3 quail that he had shot. Woohoo, supper! We went over to the Trailhead where Sue had a bonfire going. We shared our quail, salad, and pie for a good supper. It was here that I first learned of Lynx, Bernice's friend who teaches survival & primitive skills. Now this was something new!

Lynx Vilden is a primitive survival expert and a friend of Bernice's. Lynx is a Brit who moved across the pond to the USA at age 21. She runs workshops and teaches survival skills and what she calls "stone age projects." This is how our ancestors survived folks! Can you make a fire, a shelter, shoes, and find food? I could see why Bernice and Lynx became friends. Well, it seemed that Lynx was going to southern France to ride in the caves where there are pictographs of spotted horses dating back to 25,000 BC! Lynx rode and owned Appaloosa horses in northwestern US. She had asked Bernice to join her on this ride to the caves. So, Bernice began planning for this adventure, thinking about what to take.

She was going to send a box of supplies....hummm....she was going to send her propane stove and her saddle...I told her I was pretty sure that the cave dwellers did not have propane stoves nor saddles! But she packed two large boxes anyway. She was thinking about the camping in France before and after the ride with Lynx. The shipping cost about knocked Bernice off her feet, and I helped arrange a sponsor to help her out. She was comfortable with traveling by horse all over the US and Canada, but France was going to be a different experience. Bernice had an address for where to ship her supplies and she was told by Lynx where to get to and when. Remember, minimal phone contact. Seemed kind of vague to me, but what the heck, just go for it. The trip to France was in early March and this was only January, so we had a lot of adventures ahead for our winter in the southwest.

By January 3 we had returned to the Cienegas and Maternity Wells, one of our perfect camps. Water and pens on BLM land. Bernice was thinking about France now and she began going through all her gear to decide what to take to France. I went to breakfast in Sierra Vista. We had a new plan now: I had to return east to sell my house and tend to some family matters. Bernice would have me drop her in Sonoita AZ and she would ride/camp to Madrid NM, about a 400-mile ride. Laughingly, Bernice would say that I dumped her off in Sonoita! She would ride south towards Mexico, cross over into NM and head north. I would be driving north to drop all her gear at her sister's house near Albuquerque and then head east to TN and VA in my rig. I took some videos of Bernice as she rode out of the fairgrounds in Sonoita. She was comfortable in her skin to be on the road again with her horses. She had some fun adventures on that ride north. Like leaving her tent behind one place and the Border Patrol bringing it to her as she rode on!

She even got hauled a couple of times in order to save time and she met more trail angels and made new friends/fans. That is the fun of long riding, being on your horse and sleeping under the stars.

On February 11, Bella and I were reunited with Bernice. I had returned to her sister's place, and we drove north to Madrid to pick up Bernice, Spirit and Liska. We stayed at her sister's for a few days and nights. Always, Bernice in her tent. I slept in the house! We went trail riding with her sister. We enjoyed some great meals and even watched some winter olympics on TV. Modern! During the days, Bernice was packing for her upcoming trip to France. We packed two large boxes of her camping supplies and sent them off to France. At this time, we still were traveling about and riding here and there in NM. We drove south again and stayed at the Kiva Horse Motel again. Friends of mine from VA & TN joined us there. It was cold and rainy, so our time was spent taking showers, doing laundry, and using internet to blog. We headed further south to Caballo State Park. We took time to soak in the hot springs at Truth Or Consequences NM. Another friend from Pie Town came and joined us there. Bernice and I were not joined at the hip. We each did our own thing. We each had our privacy and we respected that.

Her domain was her tent and mine was my trailer. Bella went back and forth! We would chat over tea & coffee sitting outside, either soaking up sun or under cover from rain. We each retained our own identity, and our plans were made from both our inputs. Decisions were made as we moved along from place to place. Bernice almost always got in a good gallop on her horses every day. She would jump on bareback and leading Liska, off she would go. She and the horses were exhilarated when they returned.

Bernice did not have her clever tent now. It had been mailed to France! She was now in a Walmart 2-person tent! Quite a step down for her. We make do! If possible, long riders pitch their tent under cover or out of the wind if possible. Bernice sometimes pitched her tent in the horse trailer to be out of the wind. That worked! Caballo Park is along the Rio Grande river and Bernice rode the Fjords into the lake/river a couple of times. We had a mishap here: a bungee popped and the rear window of my truck shattered. That delayed our plans for a day as I had to drive to Las Cruces to get a new rear window. I even tried to catch up with my cousin in Las Cruces, but that did not happen. Bernice stayed in camp with Bella while I went to breakfast and got a new window. I also hit a Walmart in Las Cruces. My friends from back east had headed south to see White Sands & visit some friends in that area. Bernice and I headed to Silver City the next day. It was cold and wet, 38 degrees and rainy. Bernice & the Fjords stayed at the fairgrounds while I did a Motel 6 night. Bernice pitched the Walmart tent in the horse trailer to be out of the weather. We did internet at MacDonalds! The next morning, we enjoyed breakfast at Nancy's Silver Cafe in downtown Silver City and used their internet. We loaded up about noon and returned to the Gila Forest. We had made friends there back in November. Bernice got to stay in Pat's casita where she had stayed on her ride from Sonoita to Madrid! Bella and I camped at the trail head next door to our friend, Annie. I enjoyed a steak cookout and Annie's warm woodstove that evening. Bernice was working on pictures and cover designs for her book via eml at the casita. I recall Margaritas and oreo thins wrapped up the evening. It was a starry starry night! Bella's water dish froze that night!

I had a day to write some letters and pay some bills while Bernice was at the casita. The next day I picked Bernice and the Fjords up at Pat's. We headed back towards AZ, stopping at a friend's place in Safford AZ. Bernice took the horses for a gallop and I went in search of a soak in a hot spring for which this area is famous. That sure felt great. My host had made a great quiche as she has a lot of chickens! It was quite windy that night. The next day we made our way back to the Empire Ranch in the Cienegas. We camped on the airstrip, and it was a bit chilly. My VA/TN friends arrived and set up camp. All 4 of us went riding the next day. Four horses, four women riders and three happy trail dogs. We rode past huge cottonwood trees along the creeks. This ranch is beautiful. We went to the ranch headquarters and found it open, so we all got to go in and learn the history here. The movie posters are quite colorful and bring back fun memories of the western movies that we all had enjoyed in our youth. A docent gave us the speech on the history. We bought books and cards. The main house was still under reconstruction so we could not go inside. We were more interested in the barns and corrals anyway!

The local antelope herd passes through daily!

My friends headed off to Maternity Wells for some nice camping and Bernice and I got ready to head north. Bernice had a plane to catch! We got hay at the feed store in Sonoita again and headed east into NM. We camped in Socorro where Bernice felt at home having camped here in January on her ride north. Good breakfast at Sofia's in Socorro! We took some back roads and went to MountainAir, where we took some time in the National Park office. We saw some great pictures of the nearby ruins that go back to the early Spanish folk who built missions and houses here. We bought cards and mailed some from here. We got groceries at a local store. We got to Bernice's sister's place and got settled: Bernice in a tent on the deck and me in the house! The woodstove felt great! Bernice got busy pulling the shoes off the Fjords and then spent hours on her laptop, writing on her blog. Her fans need to know where she is and what she is doing!

It was here that a lady came to interview Bernice for an upcoming movie about her travels. That became an ongoing project. Bernice and I went shopping at a thrift store where she got a suitcase on wheels for $2. Perfect for her trip to France. The boxes had already arrived in France.

That evening we went out to supper and met up with some old Minnesota friends of Bernice's. The next morning it was March and 23 degrees! It was time to pack up and head north. We made it to La Junta CO that night. We would just stop along the way and let the Fjords out for a roll, pee, and graze when we felt like it. It was pretty darn windy at those fairgrounds that night. Bernice pitched the tent in the trailer. Horses were picketed. Beautiful full moon rise that night was memorable. Our destination was my friend's North Eighty Ranch in Nebraska. My horse, Maple, lived there! I have spent many a night with those friends who always welcome me. I had asked if Bernice's Fjords could stay there while Bernice went to France. Well, everyone who meets these two Fjords falls in love with them, so no problem with my friends making them feel welcome. The horses got an entire 30-acre pasture to themselves. They settled right in. It was still wintry cold, so Bernice pitched the tent in my trailer again. I slept in the house! Bella stayed with Bernice!

On March 5, 2018, Bernice took down the Walmart tent and packed it away along with all her other supplies. The Rubbermaid tubs were stored in the barn. The Fjords had settled into their paradise and France was waiting. Jeannie Grace and Rosie drove Bernice to Denver (4 hrs west). We stayed in a motel and had what we called "the last supper" with Bernice. The next morning, she took the shuttle to DIA and headed to France. We would meet up again in April. Bella and I headed back to VA to look for a house to buy. Bernice wrote about her adventure in

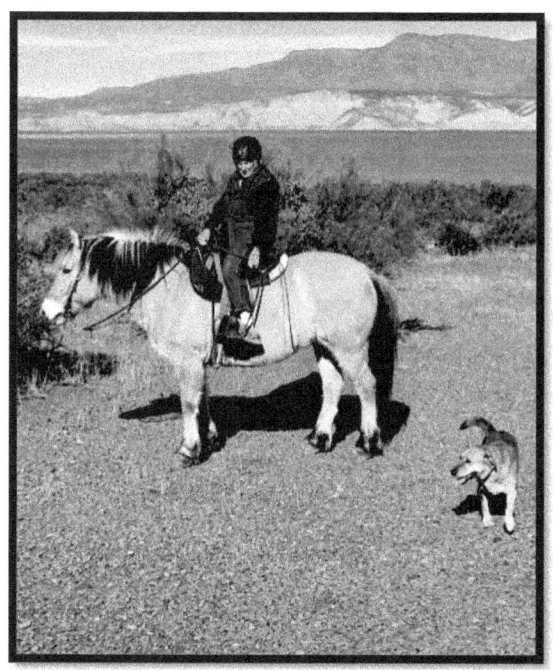

France in her blog. She told me that it was an unbelievable and unforgettable experience. Riding to the Pech Merle cave, camping out with Lynx and seeing those spotted horse drawings was like a dream. The downside of that trip was that it was cold and rainy most of the time and Bernice returned home with a bad cold but lots of memories that she would not have wanted to miss.

I returned to Nebraska on April 21, 2018. Jeannie Grace had picked Bernice up at DIA on her return. She was going to find a bus or hitchhike back to the North Eighty Ranch but was extremely grateful to see Jeannie waiting for her when she got off the plane. Poor Bernice was sick with a bad cold and felt horrible. She had lots of baggage too! Jeannie was a trail angel in disguise! I arrived just in time to hear Bernice give a 1.5 hr talk at a local cafe, MUP (Most Unusual Place) in Lewellen NE. She spoke about her long rides and her upcoming book. She answered questions from the packed house. It was a very fun gathering of folks who prefer to travel vicariously.

Local folks came to visit Bernice at the ranch. Some are owners of Fjords and wanted to see Spirit and Liska. One local family had us all over for supper as these locals had taken Bernice in during a storm when she passed through here on one of her long rides in 2008. One man had spotted her trying to get out of the horrible wind as a bad storm approached and he took her to his ranch to be safe. When I passed through that ranch several years later, they asked me if I wanted to sleep in the same room that Bernice had occupied! I said no and pitched my tent. Bernice would have been proud of me. It was not storming when I was there.

Bernice had her own tent back now and was camped in the barn to be out of the wind. April 24 was a historic day for Bernice; I drove her to Walmart where she purchased a Tracfone! Wow! She now had a cell phone so she could be in touch with her publisher and the documentary maker. She was not done her travels yet. She had plans to get to Laramie WY She and I talked over routes and dates. One problem was there was still a lot of snow on some of the high passes and she would not be able to ride through them. Nevertheless, she packed up and rode out of the

North Eighty on April 25 heading west. It was a nice sunny day as we bid her goodbye.

I caught up with Bernice again in Pine Bluffs WY as I was on my way back from a road trip to southwest CO. Bernice was staying at a small fairground for a few days. I stopped and we chatted about her trip so far. She and Bella were glad to see each other. Bernice was to have some tough riding from Pine Bluffs to Laramie through the Medicine Bow mountains. Jeannie, Bella, and I met up with her near Laramie on May 5. Bernice and the Fjords were bushed. Another friend, Barb, picked them up a few miles east of Laramie and took them to the Burns Ranch. Bernice was grateful for that and pitched her tent next to her Fjords for a rest. While there, Bernice was able to catch up on her blog and book final using Barb's internet. Also, the film lady came to video Bernice and do more interviewing for the documentary.

I returned to Laramie on May 10 to continue more travels with Bernice and the Fjords as she was having to wait for snow melt before she could continue her ride home. We set out for Colorado on May 11. At the time, I had a small cabin in CO where I used to spend my summer months with my horses. I would take Bernice there to kill time and enjoy the high country, ponderosa pines and aspens while waiting for snow to melt. Bernice pitched her tent on the porch of the cabin and the Fjords grazed the rich grass and drank from the creek. It was a fairy tale setting, off the grid, only with propane and a woodstove. We rode the horses up and down the hills and enjoyed the gorgeous views. We stayed there until May 21.

Bernice had thought that she would ride from there toward home. NO, NO! You cannot ride along US Rt 40 to Steamboat Springs! A narrow, busy mountain road with lots of traffic and no shoulder! I told her absolutely not. I would drive her to Craig where she could pick up a trail through the mountains off the road, heading northwest. Whew. So, we stayed one night at the fairgrounds in Steamboat and then went on to Craig CO the next night. We had a heck of a storm while at that fairground. On May 23 Bernice packed up the Fjords and headed northwest out of Craig heading to RockSprings WY. I bid goodbye to Lady Long Rider and that was the last time I would see her. I have a lot of pictures of her riding out on Spirit, ponying Liska with her packs loaded. From Sonoita AZ, from Lewellen NE, from Craig CO. I was still envious of Lady Long Rider!

Bernice had a sense of purpose about everything. I am a bit more spontaneous and figure that it will all work out somehow. We blended well in our travels. As we enjoyed long riding, we always experienced the same questions when camping: where will I stop, will I find water, how far should I go today, will my horse be safe tonight? The key is not to worry and let that take over the day. As Bernice would say, *"Hey, I am alive, this I know!"* We both have found peace along the way and have loved our horses and dogs.

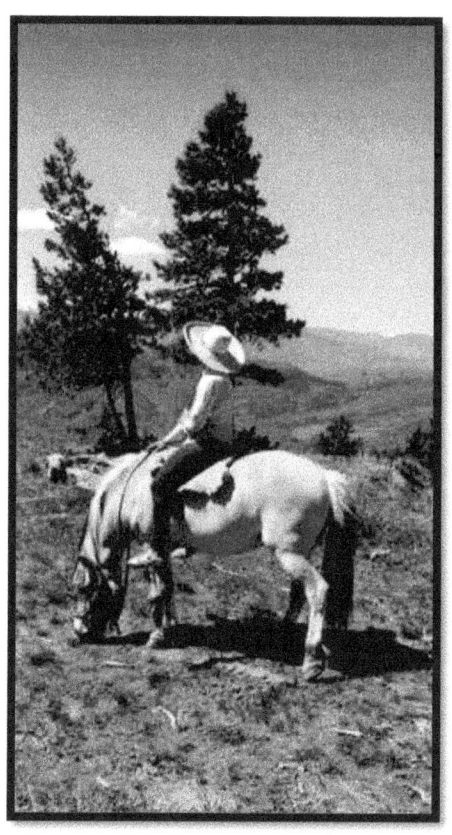

Bernice got her *"can do"* spirit from her Dad and I got the love of horses and travel from my Mom. I saw a T-shirt once that read *" To be extraordinary, you must stop being ordinary."* Bernice was extraordinary for sure. She personified the right to do what she wanted and to achieve it the best way possible. 15 years in a tent gives one time to ponder life. Bernice passed away October 2, 2021. It was an honor to call her my friend. This chapter is my tribute to Bernice.

www.ingramcontent.com/pod-product-compliance
Lightning Source LLC
LaVergne TN
LVHW061036070526
838201LV00073B/5058